IBERIAN SWORDPLAY

Domingo Luis Godinho's Art of Fencing

1599

Translation and Additional Material by
TIM RIVERA

in collaboration with
Steve Hick, Eric Myers, Manuel Valle, and Jaime Girona

Freelance Academy Press, Inc.
www.FreelanceAcademyPress.com

Freelance Academy Press, Inc., Wheaton, IL 60189
www.freelanceacademypress.com

Printed in the United States of America
by Publishers' Graphics

19 18 17 16 15 14 13 12 11 10 1 2 3 4 5

ISBN 978-1-937439-33-0
Library of Congress Control Number: 2016916100

TABLE OF CONTENTS

FOREWORD

This is a book of Destreza.

In today's world it is more common to call the fighting tradition pioneered Jerónimo Sánchez de Carranza simply "*Destreza*" but the word most correctly means skill and in this case skill at arms. The True School, or *La Verdadera Destreza*, did not have a monopoly on brilliant swordplay anymore than the Italians or Germans did. Even in his day Carranza recognized that there were wise swordsmen of the old school.

I had the experience of meeting one myself as I fenced with Tim Rivera for the first time. As we crossed blades I sensed a connection as if a long lost relative had found his way back to me; there seeing him for the first time and all his family features were plainly laid out in his smile, his laugh, and his spiraling low defensive blade actions. As martial artists our backgrounds are very dissimilar with mine being classical Italian fencing and Tim's being Filipino martial arts and yet the Iberian art we found separately was familiar and I have since taken to calling him my "brother from another book cover". By taking separate roads we had somehow come together into powerful cuts, strategies formed by domination of closed defensive lines, and similar libraries of circular actions used to control space. There were the marks of Italian sidesword present in his play but also, plain as day, the roots of the same tradition I was struggling to revive.

The western martial arts world needs this book. As a student of Carranza's True School I need to know this tradition because all the True school authors knew it. As a practitioner of Italian arts there is the promise of additional insight into the sidesword play of the masters of Southern Europe which may hold the keys to improving my own play. If you were looking for an entrance into Iberian arts, you need this book because this form of the tradition combines aspects of the True school and the Italian sidesword tradition in an approachable way. The Old School's addition of ripping play beautifully marries the power and flow of the montante with the single-handed sword.

The truth is that realizing a true *destreza*… **true skill**… is more than just comparing the dribs and drabs of technique we can harvest from the old books to realize in our art. It is the struggle to learn, to grow, to fight, and to live as best we can while we can as you walk your own road. With a sword in one hand and a book in the other you can seek to find the truth about the art and, more importantly, about yourself. It's my hope that as you walk you discover friends, brothers, and sisters on the road with you as I have.

In your hands you hold one piece of the great puzzle of *destreza*; the family of Iberian swordplay. If you dare to open the pages, if you dare to lift your sword and train, it will change you and in so doing, the world will change with you. Pause for a moment, take a deep breath, appreciate what you hold in your hands, the people living and dead that helped create this tradition and this work. When you are ready to begin, turn the page.

Puck Curtis, Maestro d'Arme
Sacramento Sword School
23 September 2016

INTRODUCTION

IBERIAN SWORDPLAY DURING THE RENAISSANCE

Renaissance Iberia (what is now Spain and Portugal) had been forged by the centuries-long *Reconquista* and saw martial exploits as central to masculine identity, so fencing was considered a crucial component of a Renaissance gentleman's education.[1] Because of this, specific systems of training and certifying fencing masters was established throughout the Iberian peninsula by the late Middle Ages, and records of fencing masters in service to the various, Iberian royal courts[2] [3] extend back to at least the early 15th century. In 1478, their Catholic Majesties Fernando and Isabella established the office of *maestro mayor* (senior master)[4] to be the chief examiner of fencing masters. The senior master was also the master to the royal pages, which indicates that it was an influential court position.[5]

The examination of fencing masters frequently involved formal boards comprised of other masters[6] and representatives of civil authority, before which the candidate who wished to prove his mastery was required to display his skill at arms and engage in a series of formal combats. Besides the sword alone (*espada sola*), these examinations could also include the two-handed sword (*montante*); sword accompanied by any number of companion arms, such as the round shield (*espada y rodela*), buckler (*broquel*), dagger (*daga*), or cloak (*capa*); two swords (*dos espadas*); dagger alone (*daga sola*); and a wide variety of polearms, such as the spear (*lanza*), half-spear, staff or stick, axe (*hacha*), or halberd (*alabarda*).

Although there are earlier records of masters and examinations, the earliest Iberian master who wrote a treatise on fencing was Jaime Pons of Perpignan.[7] He seems to have been an influential master: During one of his student's examinations in 1466, he was referred to as "the venerable master Pons,"[8] and his sons were noted as "sons of the renowned Jaime Pons" in the 1490s. His treatise was written in Catalan before or during 1474, was at least 66 folios long, and covered instruction in sword and buckler, *montante*,[9] sword and dagger, sword and cloak, dagger alone, trips and disarms, and sword alone against spear or pike. Although we have descriptions of this work, the work itself has not yet been found. According to later sources who quote him, sword and buckler appears on the first page and throughout the other pages referenced, suggesting it was possibly the primary weapon combination.[10]

Pedro de la Torre from Seville is another master, contemporary with Pons, who wrote a treatise on fencing.[11] His work also remains lost, but what we know of it from secondary sources is that it was written in 1474, was at least 124 folios long and separated into at least two parts, covering sword alone, dagger alone, sword and shield, *montante*, sword and cloak, two swords, sword and dagger, and sword against spear. Sword alone was likely the principal weapon, as it is called "the Queen of Weapons." The two-sword method was created by the author.[12]

In the following century, another famous Sevillan master, Francisco Román,[13] who was the senior master and examiner for Spain under Carlos V, authored a fencing manual in 1532 which covered at least the *montante*, sword alone, sword and shield, sword and cloak, and wrestling throws. He again refers to the sword alone as "the Queen of Weapons," but the *montante* is called "the Principal Weapon" and "the Eagle of Weapons". However, he also says that the sword and shield is best of all, and that the sword is the foundation of all shields, so it's difficult to say with certainty which weapon was his primary means of instruction.[14] As with his two predecessors, Román's work is yet to be found, although there are citations in other works.[15]

In 1583 Jeronimo Sánchez de Carranza, yet another Sevillan swordsman, published a book describing a new method of fencing, which he called *la verdadera destreza de las armas* ("the true skill of arms").[16] Carranza intended to elevate the art of fencing to a science based on geometry and Aristotelian physics, and integrated it with other subjects such as logic, philosophy, religion, music, poetry, and astrology. Carranza criticized the old style for lacking a foundation in Aristotelian thought, and rejected the label of *esgrima* ("fencing") for his art, using it as a pejorative, preferring instead to use the term *destreza*.

La verdadera destreza was initially a regional style, slowly spreading until its most prolific author, Luís Pacheco de Narváez, became senior master of Spain in 1624.[17] Although the rivalry between the two methods would continue into the next century, the old style was gradually consumed by the new requirements for master certification and a deluge of published works on *la verdadera destreza*. These authors used various, perjorative labels for the old style: *esgrima común* ("common fencing"), *esgrima vulgar* ("vulgar fencing"), *esgrima antigua* ("old fencing"), *destreza ordinaria* ("ordinary skill"), *destreza antigua* ("old skill"), *destreza vulgar* ("vulgar skill"), and *destreza falsa* ("false skill").

DOMINGO LUIS GODINHO AND THE OLD STYLE

In 1599, during the period of time in which the Portuguese crown was united with the crown of Castile and Aragon, a Portuguese fencing master named Domingo Luis Godinho wrote a manuscript in Spanish entitled *Arte de Esgrima* ("Art of Fencing"). It was never published, and next to nothing is known about the life of the author, apart from being a native of Santarem.[18] The treatise is significant in that it is the first complete treatise discovered which describes the older style of swordsmanship. As of this writing, the only other known work (aside from lists of *montante* rules) is a Spanish manuscript fragment dating to 1580,[19] which appears to be a transcription of two paragraphs of an older work. There is no reference to the title, author, or date of the original, but it bears a strong resemblance to the method described by Godinho.

One of the characteristics ascribed by later authors to the old style is a foundation based on "nails-up" and "nails-down" hand positions.[20] [21] In the same way, Godinho establishes his primary position or *guard* by describing the point of the sword pointed to the enemy, with the hand either nails-up or nails-down. He also describes various postures that depart from this by raising or lowering the sword, provoking the opponent to attack into the openings created, which he then describes how to counter. Pacheco says Román called it "inviting the opponent" (*incitar o llamar al contrario*), though Pons was the first to write about it.[22] As both a counter and an attack, Godinho describes a thrust to the hand,[23] which Pacheco says only de la Torre approved of and wrote about.[24] Against a nails-up thrust on the inside, one of the most frequent counters described by Godinho is called "thrusting by the same edges" (*punta por los mismos filos*), which de la Torre also advised, calling it "wounding by the same attack" (*herir por el mismo acometimiento*); finally, Pacheco also describes thrusting by the edges in his depiction of common Spanish fencing.[25]

Godinho's method of fighting with other weapon combinations is built on the foundation of the sword alone. With sword and shield, Godinho says that all attacks are better given low,[26] which is the same advice attributed to Pons and Román.[27] With sword and dagger against sword alone, Godinho says that it is best to parry with the sword and wound with the dagger,[28] which de la Torre also advises.[29] Fighting with two swords is taught by way of *reglas* ("rules"), which are a series of sword movements and accompanying footwork which can be performed as a solo exercise and is designed to be performed repeatedly in a particular fighting context. Godinho's rules for fighting with two swords share many of the same contexts and movements as the *montante.* His first two-sword rule is a *reves* with the left sword, followed by a *tajo* with the right.[30] According to Pacheco, de la Torre (who claims to have invented his method of fighting with two swords) describes a similar movement of parrying with the left sword and wounding the left arm with the right sword.[31]

There were said to be seven, universal or core *montante* rules before being expanded by Román to include contexts such as fighting in narrow or wide streets.[32] Godinho also gives rules for *montante* use in specific, tactical contexts such as facing another *montante,* fighting in a narrow street, fighting surrounded in a wide street, an intersection of four streets, the center of a plaza, while facing two shieldmen, while guarding a lady or cloak, and how to use the montante to separate a fight.[33] The twelve rules of Pablo de Paredes, the senior master of Spain in 1599, contains many of the same contexts, including making space, fighting in a narrow street, guarding a cloak, a round plaza, and a wide street.[34] Pacheco also says that fencers of the old-style make a horizontal cut to the legs with the *montante* against two shieldmen,[35] which is Godinho's fifth rule.[36]

All of these similarities between Godinho's work, Paredes' rules, and Pacheco's descriptions of 15th-century fencing texts suggest that the Portuguese master was very much continuing a style of combat that had preceded him for at least a century.

ABOUT THE TEXT

The only known exemplar of *Arte de Esgrima* is in the rare books and manuscripts section of the *Biblioteca Nacional de Lisboa* (National Library of Lisbon), coming from the library of the Marquis of Pombal. The manuscript contains 133 numbered leaves of paper bound in parchment. Leaves 2, 4, and 8 are missing, and the numbering skips 61, giving the final folio as number 137. It has been cited by Moniz (58), Sousa Viterbo (XX), Leguina (73) and Valle (188).

The treatise itself begins on folio 12,[37] is divided into chapters, and is not illustrated. It begins with sword alone, and includes shield, buckler, two swords, sword and dagger, *montante*, cloak, and a chapter covering techniques "against treachery," comprised of various sneak-attacks and dirty play. It then introduces a few more general chapters on fencing, before continuing with more chapters for the sword alone. The first eleven folios consist of various tables and lists of topics in the treatise, many containing check marks or notes on page or chapter; also contained within are a series of numbered paragraphs that briefly discuss a particular point.

WEAPONS

Sword (*Espada*)

When speaking of the one-handed sword, Godinho doesn't speak of any particular style of weapon, and his method only relies on the presence of a crossguard, such as had been in use for centuries. However, the typical sword of late 16th-century Iberia has a straight, double-edged blade around 80 - 100 cm (31.5 - 39.5 in) in length, with a width of 3 - 4 cm (1.2 - 1.5 in). Beyond this, tastes varied; some preferred the older blade style, which was slightly wider and shorter, while some preferred a longer, narrow blade, similar to what we associate today with the "rapier". In fact, various royal decrees in the 16th century made it illegal to possess a sword with a blade longer than five-fourths of a *vara* (about 105 cm, or 41 in).

The sword's guard typically consisted of a cross, whether straight or curved, along with finger rings, side rings or posts, and a knuckle guard. Hilts consisting of multiple complicated rings and sweeping loops was a new development during the 16th century, and was becoming popular by the end of the century. Again, tastes varied, with the older, simpler styles persisting and being used along with the newer styles.

Also developed during this century was a practice sword with no edge and a button point; it was referred to as the *espada negra* (black sword), in contrast to the sharp sword, or *espada blanca* (white sword).

Shield (*Rodela*) and Buckler (*Broquel*)
The word *rodela* refers to a round shield, typically around 62 cm (24 in) across, strapped to the arm. Historically, many were curved, made of steel with rolled edges, but some were flat, made of wood and faced with leather. In contrast, the buckler is a small round shield between 25 - 36 cm (10 - 14 in) in diameter, and was always gripped in the center by a single hand grip, protected by a small dished area called a "boss".

Dagger (*Daga*)
The typical dagger of the period had a straight blade with two edges, and could be quite long, anywhere between 24 and 36 cm (9.5 - 18 in) in overall length. The hilt styles generally follow those of swords, though less elaborate and lacking finger rings.

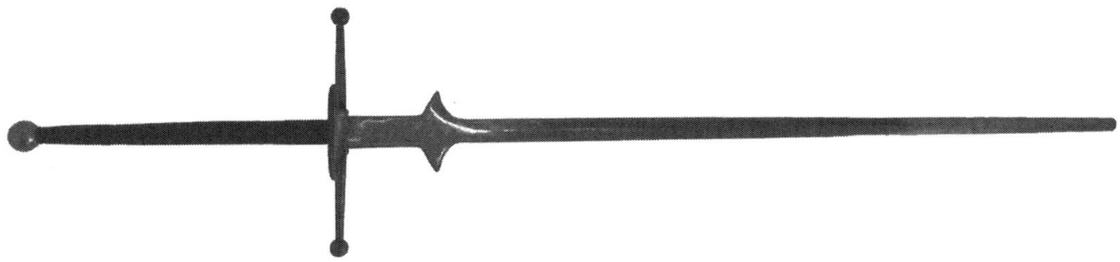

Two-Handed Sword (*Montante*)
The two-handed sword is described by Pacheco as being six Castilian feet (1.67 m / 5.5 ft) long, with one quarter of that being the length of the hilt, and weighing around 2.25 kg (5 lbs). The hilts nearly always consist of a straight cross, with or without additional side rings. The *montante* came to widespread use in the 16th century, but ceased battlefield use in the next century. It became associated with fencing masters, and its image was used as a badge of office.

Godinho advises that because of the weapon's length, it should be carried in the hand, in a position similar to a modern "shouldered arms" with a rifle:

> *Because of that, I suggest that at night, the montante is carried without a sheath, and the wielder without a cloak, and the montante in the left hand, tilted diagonally, and not on the back as many carry it.*

A similar carrying position is illustrated several decades later by the Italian master, Francesco Alfieri in *Lo Spadone* (1653).

A PRIMER FOR INTERPRETING GODINHO'S ART OF FENCING

Godinho's method doesn't adhere to a strict form, and as such, the treatise does not begin with instruction on basics such as postures, footwork, or how to grip the sword. Instead, he scatters notes on these topics throughout the text. In order to make it easier to follow along with the text, much of this advice has been collected and presented here.

How to Grip the Sword

There is no specific way to grip the sword in Godinho's method; he says that whichever way is most natural for the person holding the sword is the best – even if it's in the left hand. This view on left-handedness is significant, as being left-handed was seen as an ignoble quality and was very strongly discouraged among the Spanish nobility. Authors of works on *la verdadera destreza* go so far as to ignore the issue of left-handedness altogether, simply requiring students to fence right-handed.

Some ways to grip the sword include wrapping one, two, or no fingers around the cross, having the thumb touching the fingers, or straight along the *recazo*.

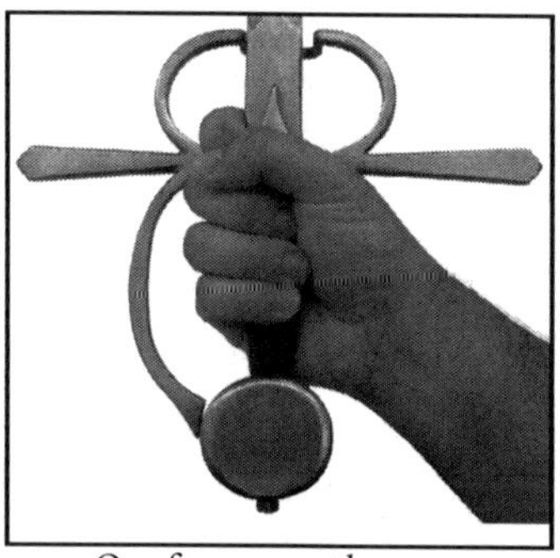
One finger over the cross

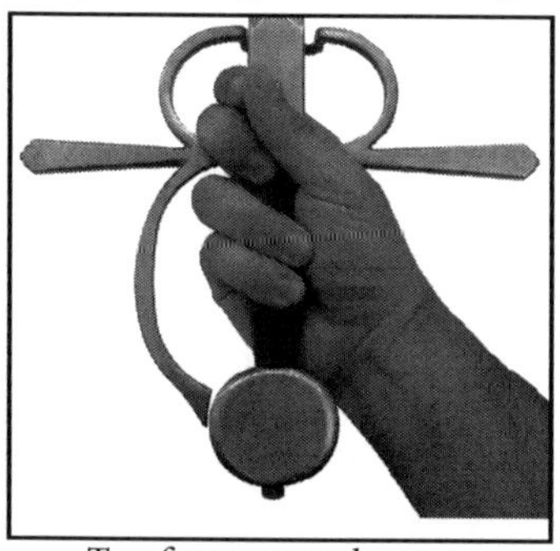
Two fingers over the cross

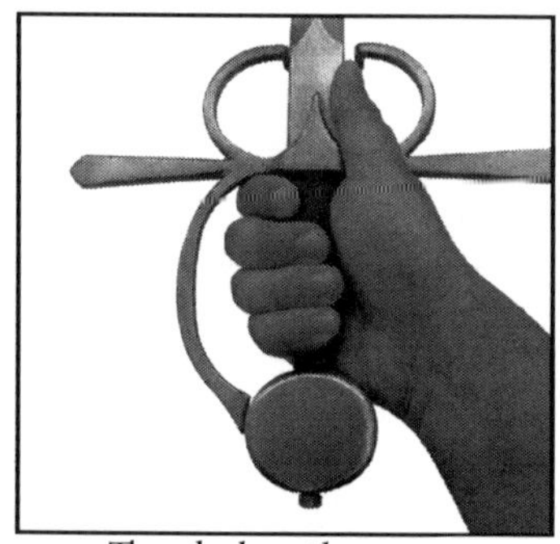
Thumb along the recazo

Nails-Up and Nails-Down

Rather than a system "guard positions," the author details two positions in which the hand will almost always be placed: nails-up (hand in supination) and nails-down (hand in pronation). In these positions, the blade should be flat with the crosses pointing left and right. Turning the hand between these two positions should be done by simply turning the wrist and arm (with possible lateral movement of the hilt), while keeping the movement of the sword's point to a minimum.

Nails-Down

Nails-Up

Footwork and Posture

Godinho indicates that the precise placement of the feet varies based on circumstance, and that a good posture is simply that which avoids the opponent's blow. In many chapters, a bit of advice is given on the particular movement of the feet or body for that situation, but most chapters say nothing on the subject. However, a few general guidelines and recurring footwork patterns are noted here.

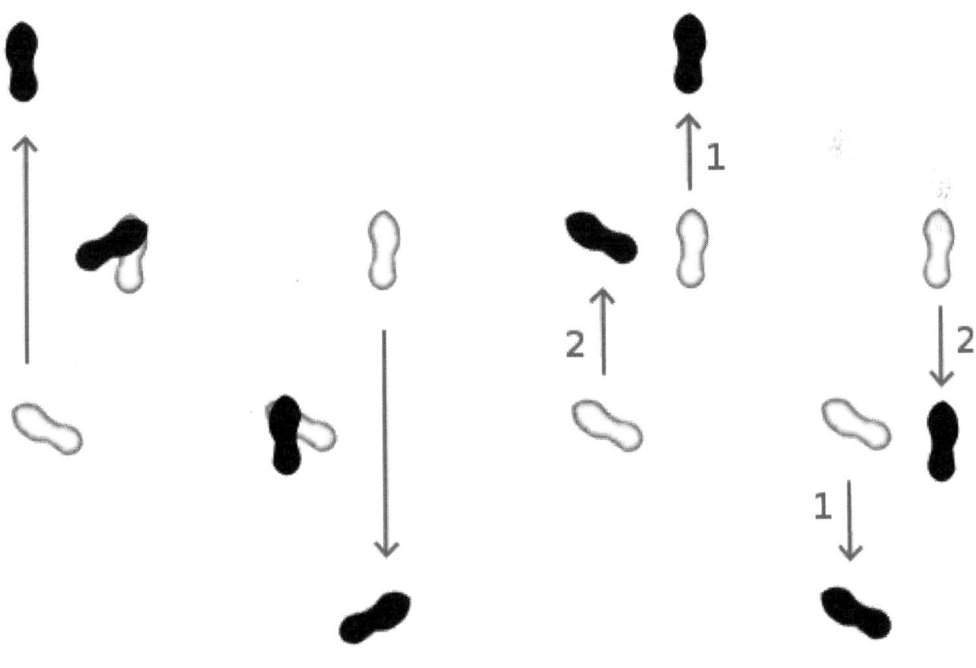

Footwork Diagram: natural walk and keeping the right in front

In general, the body should be held in an upright posture, and paces should be as close as possible to a natural walk. Alternatively, the right foot can always be kept in front of the left – when stepping forward, the step should be made first with the right, with the left following; when stepping back, the left foot steps back first, and the right follows.

There are many other steps in the text which aren't as common, but three of them merit discussion here:

- A **wheeling step**, is done with the right foot in front; the left foot crosses behind the right foot to the right side, which results in almost turning your back to the opponent.
- A **turn** is common in the rules for two swords and *montante*, and is used to turn completely around and face the opposite direction. This is done with either foot in either direction.
- A **double step**, calls for the rear foot to step to the side and then immediately step forward. These last two types of footwork are specifically used when dealing with multiple opponents.

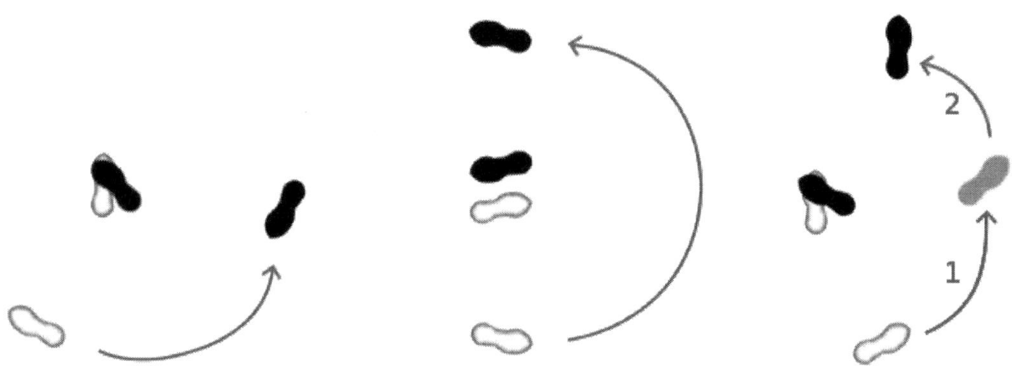

Footwork Diagram: Wheeling Step, Turn, Double Step

Distance

Godinho advises an honest measure to begin is the distance at which the opponent's sword cannot reach without stepping, the point falling one or two palms (8 - 16 in, 20 - 40 cm) short of contact.

Honest Measure: Opponent cannot reach without a step

Established

This only applies to what is called **established play** (*afirmado*), where a fencer places his sword in a position (usually nails-up or nails-down) and does not move his feet, waiting for the correct moment to strike, counter, or commit some other technique. In contrast, there is **ripping play** (*rasgado*), wherein the fencer keeps his sword in motion, delivering cuts and thrusts, while stepping. When the fencer in ripping play has the opportunity to attack or defend, he converts the current motion of the sword to the appropriate strike, parry, or counter needed at the time.

Shield Positions

The default position for the shield is with the left arm rounded, the shield being one palm distant from the chest, covering only the left side. This is the same whether armed nails-up or nails-down. When parrying to the left side, the shield is held on the left side of the head, such that the opponent can be seen past the right side of the shield. When parrying to the right, the shield is passed to the left side, so that the opponent can be seen past the left side of the shield, and the left foot is forward. Low sword parries are made in such a way that the shield protects the hand.

The sword hand is turned nails-up with the point low, and the nails of the shield hand touch the nails of the sword hand to parry left; the position to parry right is identical, but with the sword hand turned nails-down (still being covered by the shield).

Most common way to position the shield

Parry to the right side

Parry to the left side

Low parry to the right side

Parry to the left side

Low parry to the right side

Low parry to the left side

Holding the buckler, arm-extended at all times.

Godinho has little to say about the buckler, but is explicit that the buckler arm is held fully extended, and the right foot is kept in front. With the *montante*, there are no explicit guards, although Rule 1 does refer to the nails-up and nails-down positions from sword alone, and we are told to grip the *montante* with the right hand near the guard and the left near the pommel.

TRANSLATOR'S NOTES

Translating Godinho's *Art of Fencing* presents several interesting challenges. The manuscript itself is far from polished, appearing to be a rough draft bound to a collection of his notes. There are words crossed out, having been written by mistake or as a reminder crossed off a list. The writing borders on the illegible in many instances. Combined with the document's age, water damage, and stray marks, this caused the transcription itself to be very difficult.[38]

The text is written primarily in Spanish, although it contains many elements of orthography and vocabulary from Portuguese. Godinho occasionally refers to Portuguese as "the other language," giving the Portuguese translation of a particular word. As they both translate to the same in English, these portions have been moved to footnotes.

There is virtually no punctuation in the original, only an occasional hyphen and erratic use of *interpuncts* to separate words or groups of words. Punctuation has been added to this translation for ease of readability; additionally, in many cases the tense of the verbs has been changed from future perfect or future conditional, to the simple present tense, since neither are used to convey instructions in modern English and read awkwardly without conveying any additional nuance of meaning.

A handful of terms have not been translated to English. Although a full treatment of these terms is given in the glossary, a brief footnote giving a sense of the word is given the first time it is encountered in the text. These terms were not translated either because a simple translation was either too general or misleading. Rather than create new English jargon, the words have been left as they are written in the original and italicized.

Conversely, some other terms have been given an English translation, but are also marked with a footnote at their first appearance, giving the original word in italics. They are given an entry in the glossary because either because Godinho defines them as technical terms, or because the choice of words for their translation into English calls for a bit of explanation. Some of them also have nuances of meaning that are lost when rendered into English, and understanding these alternative meanings will help the reader better understand the art.

THE ART OF FENCING
DOMINGO LUIS GODINHO
1599

PART ONE: SWORD ALONE

IHS MA

With the name of Jesus and his blessed mother, the book called Art of Fencing begins, composed by Master Domingo Luis Godinho, native Lusitanian[40] from the town of Santarem, diocese of Lisbon. – D. in the year 1599

f.12 Francisco de Acevedo[39]

Chapter One: On the Three General Rules and Dealing with the Counters

What must first be advised to those that will learn this art with curiosity, is that its masters declare three general rules to their disciples, whereby he who plays with the sword alone can easily gain knowledge of it. The first rule is that every time a person is attacked on the right side by his opponent, whether by any thrust or a *reves*,[42] it has to be defended with a fingernails-down thrust. The second is that every time that one is attacked on the left side, whether by a *tajo*[43] or any thrust, it has to be defended fingernails-up. The third is that one not only has to be defend by parrying, but with the said thrusts injuring the enemy, noting that the thrust has to be given to where the opponent's blow is going to stop, in this manner: if the opponent's *reves* goes to the head, the counter thrust is given to the face or the shoulder, and if the *reves* or thrust goes to the thigh, the counter thrust is given in the opponent's thigh, and if the *tajo* or thrust goes to the face, the counter should also go to the opponent's face or chest. In conclusion, the third rule is that the counters have to be given at the height where the opponent's blow goes.

honor and benefit is intended in weapons and life ...[41]

that the blows have to be offensive and defensive

advise those that he will examine that they are not reckless in play, etc.

it is enough if many evils can be

fisherman surrounded by water

The poultice is placed on the wound[44]

Chapter Two: How the Opponent Is Attacked

The previous chapter deals with the form in which the counters have to be given, but it doesn't speak of how the enemy will be attacked — for that, one would do well to keep to the third rule. The posture and height in which the opponent is positioned has to be noted, such that if his point is in front of your face, you commit whichever blow to the opponent's face. So in this manner, you have to commit the blow at whichever height it may be. The movements and swaying of the body with which one commits these blows is not dealt with in this chapter, because they will be declared in their place.

f.13

Chapter Three: How to Draw, Against One and Against Two, Close or Far

Two people meet close to each other, and at an end of their words have to draw swords. As they draw, they take the right foot back with the whole body, remaining nails-down. If they aren't far enough from each other, they may then take back the left foot. Then one puts in the left foot with a *tajo*, which the opponent receives nails-up, giving a thrust to the face or chest, turning himself to the side the most that he will be able. He will also be able, in place of the *tajo*, to give a nails-up thrust, putting in said left foot; I mean to say, entering with the right foot. The opponent will be able to defend the nails-up thrust with a thrust by the same edges.

and the nails-up thrusts will be committed like this

Chapter Four: How the Steps are Done Against One

the step has to originate with the raised foot.

the body and foot have to go back when they retreat

that it is false to necessarily enter with the left foot

Standing with the feet together, and lifting the sword with vigor, the disciple puts in the left foot with a *tajo*, then enters with the right foot with a *reves*, and a *tajo* like the first, and he goes with this step, walking until it is sufficient. Retreating, the left foot leaves nails-up and the right foot nails-down, such that one parries the opponent's *tajos* and *reveses*, because taking the crossing parries is not as effective.[45] The steps that one makes are not big, but like those that he makes when he walks.

Second Step Against Many

that in a battle one is not able to keep step, another step is made with the right foot

He will also be able to throw a *tajo* with the right foot forward, if the left foot does not pass ahead of the right. Walking like this with the right foot always in front, he cuts the *tajo* and *reves*. If it would be necessary to retreat, it is with the left foot back first and the right after, not passing beyond the left, but after it. With this step he should go exiting in the above form, nails-up thrust to those on the left side and nails-down thrust to those on the right side.

f.14

Chapter Five: How to Cut

the left foot doesn't have a certain place

Done with the step, the disciple stands feet together, and putting in the right foot, he makes a *tajo*, extending as much as he is able, and when the *tajo* withdraws, he withdraws the foot that he had placed at the same time, returning it to where it began. Then he returns to put in a *reves*, extending it as much as he is able, and as the *reves* passes, he withdraws the foot like he withdrew for the *tajo*. Then he puts in a *tajo* with the left foot. If there is more than one opponent, then when he puts in the left foot, it should not be straight from the other, but to the left side so that it reaches more. Then in this form, he puts in the right foot with a *reves*, and cuts with this step as much as necessary, taking note that the eyes should always go where the blow goes.

why the foot is withdrawn

here two points are shown

Being necessary to retreat, he should leave by placing the feet with the same step, giving a nails-up thrust to parry those on the left side, and a nails-down thrust to those on the right side, not making a circle with his sword when he turns the sword from nails-up to nails-down, only turning with the wrist.

and the body straight

Chapter Six: How One Cuts Against Many on a Wide Street

If one is attacked in a wide street, or unable to reach all the opponents with the blows pointed out in the previous rule,[46] he will put his right foot toward those on the right side and throw a *tajo*, which will cut until reaching those that are on the left side. At the same time that the *tajo* cuts, he lifts the right foot and puts it in front of the left foot. Then, he puts the left foot to the left side, giving a *reves* to those on the same side, which will cut until reaching those on the right side. He goes when the *reves* cuts. At the same time that the reves cuts, he will lift the left foot and put it in front of the right foot.

and draw against many

Note that when you finish the *tajo*, and you want to arm the *reves*, incline the point[47] nails-up at those remaining to the right side, which is not in order to injure, as much as for the parry of the blows that the opponents may throw in the time that the *tajo* passes. Time isn't lost because in order to give the *reves*, one ends with the point already armed.

Note: arm with the point nails-up

f.15

When you finish the *reves*, and you want to give the *tajo*, you have to turn the point nails-down to those that remain to the left side, not so that you injure with it, but for parrying the blows that the opponents will give as soon as the *reves* passes, and at the same time, the *tajo* is armed with the said point. With this step, you will make the blows that will be necessary, taking note that the body should always go straight, where the blow goes, with your eyes on the opponents.

arm point nails-down

two remedies

Being necessary to retreat, rip[48] with *reves* and *tajo*, or give a nails-up thrust as a parry to those on left side and a nails-down thrust to those on the right side.

Chapter Seven: How to Rip and What It Is

Breaking and ripping[49] are the same thing.[50] When in battle, if the opponent on one side lowers his sword until it is in front of the belt, and he is attacked with a thrust to the eyes, this can be ripped, along with all the other [attacks] that would be committed at the time that the opponent has his sword low.

the same can be done to whichever thrust

one has to be nails-up in order to rip with a *reves* and nails-down in order to rip with a *tajo*

In order to rip, one has to be nails-down; then, lifting the sword suddenly, it meets with the enemy's sword, and at the same time he delivers a ripped *tajo* from the enemy's left shoulder to the right knee, the sword ending nails-up on the left side. Then, lifting the sword suddenly, it meets the same sword and at the same time he gives a *reves*, making a circle, from the right shoulder to the left knee. All the times that he finishes ripping, he ends armed nails-up with the sword high.

Chapter Eight: What Qualities the Player Has to Have

that has to give different plates

high

f.16

measure[51]

The master has to advise the disciple that he should be gallant, graceful, lively, nimble, spirited, and long in the postures, and he should go straight with the body. When committing the blows, he should keep the arm long, not withdrawn, nor moving more than enough for his blow to reach, except when the nails-down thrusts are given in the form that will be dealt with ahead, which gives license to enter.

by the signs, the air is known

Before one delivers a blow, he should not make any movement with the body that it naturally wants to do, but instead throw it when it is conceived in thought, and without fear, since the blow is never executed by giving everything, but by always being defended. All the times that one would have to be armed, he does so far from the opponent, and comes to him so that the swords do not reach much more than one or two palms[52] in front of the point. The times one has to attack should be the step that is suitable for each blow, as will be dealt with ahead. In play, he is restrained, and even though the bout goes wrong, he doesn't show himself as passionate, and the master intends that they [the students] do not leave angry, but as friends, nor does he allow them to depart from the rule of his lessons – take note that one never commits a blow twice in a bout.

and there is no friendship in that

How to Take the Sword from the Floor, and How to Set It Down When the Bout Is Finished

He that will enter a bout, before he removes the cloak or the sword, will lower himself to take the practice sword[53] with which he will battle, before he removes the cloak or the sword without removing the hat. Removing his cloak, sword, dagger, and other arms that he has brought, he will come to the opponent and they will both cross swords. This crossing made, they will remove their hats. As soon as they has done this, they will start their bout, and it is finished when they would settle.[54] One that will settle brings both feet together and will play a very long *tajo*, putting in the right foot, so that he is completely encircled by the sword, then withdrawing said foot to where it began. Then, putting in the left foot, he will throw a very long *reves*. When arming this *reves*, the sword should be placed in front in the manner of a nails-up thrust, and the *reves* that he will play turns all the way to the other side, and then taking back the left foot that had been placed, brushing it against the floor. Making a salute,[55] he lowers the sword arm to the floor and arms it nails-up, placing the sword on the floor, and taking his hat and other items — One can also settle by throwing a *tajo* low to the floor that ends with point nails-up, putting in the right foot. Then he should throw a low *reves* that doesn't reach to the head, nor even to the left arm, putting in the left foot, and the *reves* ends nails-down. This *reves* and *tajo* can be given without putting in either foot. Finished making his salute, he puts down the sword and take his hat.

they will take them off, put them back on, and turn to part

f.17

and also putting in one and the other

Take note that if the party remains aggrieved from the bout, one should not let go of the practice sword[56] after settling until he takes his cloak and sword, and after being taken, he returns to put the practice sword in its place.

Chapter Nine: What Nails-Down and Nails-Up Means

The disciple has an obligation to know what is meant by nails-down and nails-up. When this is said, it is understood that they will speak of the fingernails of the hand. When nails-down is said, the fingernails have to be turned well down such that the crosses remain with one of

the sword hand

to the floor

the points to the right side and the other to the left side, no more or less. When nails-up is said, they have to be turned such that they are turned well to the sky, the crosses remaining as we say above.

Chapter Ten: What Is Tajo, Reves, Freeing, Garatusa, Mandoble, Gaining, Testing, and Wrist

The master has an obligation to declare to his disciples in words and doctrine the particular causes and names that are given to the arms, and to make them informed of all before he puts them in play.

Tajo is a blow that is necessarily given to the opponent's left side, and *reves* a blow that is given to the right side.

another freeing is dealt with ahead

Freeing[57] is when the opponent goes to undo the blow that they bring to injure, with such awareness and readiness that the opponent does not meet the sword.

f.18

Garatusa is when two are established[58] nails-up, one of them in this same posture gains the opponent's sword from above, well along the length, and goes twisting the hand in a manner that his sword gives a turn around the opponent's.

the wheel of the mill

Mandoble is that whenever the two cross low, one of them turns with a *reves* to the opponent's head; the arm does not lift, only the wrist.

Wrist is when the blows that have to be given with the strength of the arm are given by only twisting the hand with the muscles that are between the hand and the arm.

Testing[59] is when, the two being established, the opponent brings the point of his sword to the point of the opponent's.

Gaining[60] is when my sword comes to the middle of the enemy's sword, taking control.

Chapter Eleven: On the Qualities of a Master

they do not have to be easily thrown into play

With much good reason, the masters that profess this art, aware of both its worth and that of the illustrious people they communicate and deal with, do much to comply with due honor to the fame, recognition, and other things that cause a reputation, which at times is worth more for a good master than being very skilled in the art. They should not be expected to give play to anyone, but to another master like themselves, an examined fencer, or a knight, where it would result in honor to themselves.

playing is mechanical, understanding is a liberal art

water surrounded

the players surround the water like fishermen

The master should be thought of in a way that the disciples have respect for him, without the rudeness seen in many masters, who personally set a bad example. By not lacking skill[61] and dealing truthfully with them, he should teach the truth of the play, to the best of his knowledge, even though the price that has been paid is low, because his conscience is obligated to do all this. His house should be a school of arms, not of cards or other illicit things. He should declare to his disciples the dangers in all the blows that the opponent can aim at him, not leave them blind and without counters. Counters should be defensive at the same time, and the attacks[62] given in such a manner that they are at the same time defensive, in a manner that isn't ruled by the popular opinion that says it is good to receive a cut in order to give a thrust. Because I have more obligation to save my own person than to kill the other; it's more valuable to leave the fight sound than to wound the other, and myself along with him.

although the price is low

f.19

mainly because as many die from a cut as a thrust

In this manner, the blows that the master teaches, as well as their counters, are offensive and defensive at the same time. He neither consents to nor approves of the play called *brazal*,[63] since it is not truly safe, nor a play that belongs in sword alone.

Chapter Twelve: On the Qualities of the Disciple

If it is true that those persons that have received some education from others, like reading, playing an instrument, accounting, etc., have a natural obligation to be gracious, grateful, and respectful of their teachers all their lives,[64] there is so much more reason to do so toward the master from whom they have learned an art so natural and honorable to man as the defense of his life. Because of that, the disciples must ensure their master's honor in everything, not only at that time that they are learning from him, but all their lives; not looking to the master's faults, if he has them, but to the obligation of disciple to master, and in all occasions, using good words to defend his honor and person.

Chapter Thirteen: Why Fencing Bouts are Arranged and How They are Done

I have said, according to my weak understanding, that as a performer has an obligation to rehearse alone many times before representing the work in public, it seems that if one is certain and tuned in to the truth when alone, they can trust those that touch the honor of it, that going out in public, they will do so with honor. Likewise, neither more nor

f.20

less, I take care that the public play of the arms is truly a fight when it happens by chance, and that those that who profess arms need to be rehearsed like performers, so that having occasion to fight, they are skilled[65] and capable of that which their masters have taught them. This rehearsal is for someone who has arranged to have the bouts, so that in being exercised with the habit of them, they go ready in what they have learned from their masters; using neither clubbing blows nor bad blows, striving to be well-defended from the opponent's blows where he finds them uncovered, whether attending to the parries or the uncovered techniques,[66] and other circumstances necessary to [the display of] skill,[67] obeying when the master puts in the *montante* and orders them to settle,[68] turning to him as has been seen, which is certainly not in order to praise, but to reprove.[69]

though before he puts it in, only to the word

Chapter Fourteen: On the Abbreviations in This Book

The reader should note[70] that where he will find Us, it means nails-up, and where he will find Ub, that it means nails-down. Where he will find a T, it means *tajo*, and where he will find an R, it means *reves*. Where he will find a P, it means thrust, and where he will find a G, it means *garatusa*, and where he will find an M, it means *mandoble*.

15 – 1599

Chapter Wherein Begins the Sword Alone, from the Postures of Nails-Up and Nails-Down, Tajo, Reves, Mandoble, Garatusa, Play for Lefties, Balanzadas, Manoplados, Tricks,[71] and Doubled Lessons. 1599

f.21

blows that originate from the nails-up posture

that the counters go at the same time

The two established nails-up, if one of them lowers the sword, the opponent may commit a nails-up thrust to the eyes. If they will defend it with the same edges by another nails-up thrust, turn the hand nails-down, inclining the right shoulder to the left side, and give the nails-down thrust in the same place where you committed the nails-up thrust. Take note that here you do not make two stops, but one. For the opponent to free the said nails-up thrust by the same edges, he cannot continue to gain the other sword. If one will gain it the moment he goes nails-up, he can easily give the thrust in the right shoulder more outside than inside. As he gains the other's sword and finds it nails-down, his sword leaves from the shoulder. Because of that, when he runs with the nails-up thrust, the opponent can easily turn the hand nails-down and give the thrust very well. Take note that when one goes with the nails-up thrust, it has to be truly executed and not just threatened, because threatening is something else.

Chapter Sixteen, About the Same Thrust

At the time that the opponent is attacked with a nails-up thrust, if he doesn't defend it by the same edges, but by pressing on it and gaining the sword in the middle, turning the hand with the wrist, he frees below, and going around the hand, gives a *tajo* in to the face.

Note that after the opponent has gone to gain your sword, it doesn't take place because you leave with the said *tajo* when the opponent presses, in a manner leaving the *tajo* executed and the enemy tricked. You will be able to do the same when the opponent presses on your sword — in place of the above *tajo*, give a nails-down thrust in the belly, entering somewhat, leaving then with *tajo* and *reves*, taking the foot back.

Note the freeing below, that it is not that which is practiced

Chapter Seventeen

Established nails-up, or in whichever manner that the two will be, if the opponent throws a descending *tajo*, wait for it with a nails-up thrust to the quillons hand. Take note that it is nails-up because, in missing the thrust, the parry is made in the quillons. If the opponent throws a *reves* to the head, wait for it with a nails-down thrust to said quillons. Note that it is nails-down because if the thrust misses, the parry is made in the quillons. This same thrust can be given when the two are established, the opponent turning the hand nails-up with a thrust in the quillons hand; at the time that the opponent throws said thrust, it is contradicted by lowering the arm and putting in a foot as much as necessary to reach with a nails-down thrust in the belly, or by lifting the hand when the opponent commits said thrust, then putting in

f.22

good for armored

if the arm retreats, nails-up thrust to the chest

the foot with a nails-down thrust in the chest, lifting the arm.

Chapter Eighteen

After the two are established, if one of them lowers the sword, the opponent gives him a *tajo* into the crook of the sword arm's elbow, while retreating backwards. If he moves against it with a nails-up thrust on the left side, the opponent defends it with a nails-up thrust by the same edges. If he moves on the right side, the opponent defends it with a nails-down thrust. In all, keep to the general rule of the first chapter. Note that elsewhere the left side is called *inside* and the right side is called *outside.*

Chapter Nineteen

putting in and withdrawing the foot

After being established nails-up, if the opponent sees him preparing a nails-up thrust at the time that he lowers [his point], he rips with a *tajo*, cutting from the left shoulder to the right knee. This *tajo* can be defended with a nails-up thrust at the eyes, committing it from the side, taking the blow in the quillons with the hand high, so that the head stays behind it, and the body is removed as much as possible.

f.23

Chapter Twenty

note that as you see these rules beginning in the same manner, in the end they are different, and not being so, they would not be perfect

The two are established nails-up with the swords together. The opponent may put the right foot suddenly to the enemy's right side with much speed, and turning the hand nails-down at the same time, gives a thrust in the eyes, with the opponent's sword remaining over the crook of his elbow. Take note that moving, putting in the foot, and giving the thrust all has to be in one single time.

The true counter of this thrust is that, as the opponent begins, the enemy gives a *balanzada*, lowering to his left side and thrusting nails-down to the opponent's belly, moving in as much as he is able.

another counter

But at the time that the opponent commits said thrust, if the enemy retreats rearward, nails-up, the opponent may continue toward him with the same nails-up thrust by the same edges.

another

If the enemy does not retreat, but lowers his sword's point, gain it in the quillons and give him a nails-up thrust.

If the opponent presses the sword on the left side as he is attacked with the thrust, give him a nails-down thrust in the belly with speed and, if it will be possible, free so that the sword doesn't meet it.

and if he presses on the sword, give a nails-down thrust in the belly as follows

Chapter Twenty-One

Being established nails-up, the swords placed such that one comes to the middle of the other, one of them may turn the point of his sword to the point of the opponent's sword with much speed, not so that the points come together, but so that it goes above. Going around above the same point, his right arm gains the point of the opponent's sword: Leaving, going below said arm, remaining outside of it. At the same time, he puts his left foot to the side and twists the hand, giving a nails-down thrust in the face. If the enemy puts in his foot before the sword passes, the opponent can give him a nails-up thrust in the left shoulder. If it happens that the opponent is so fast that the sword passes before he gives said counters, he will give another nails-up thrust in the face while turning the right foot back.

f.24
if putting in the foot more than extending the arm

Chapter Twenty-Two

Established nails-up, if one of the two lowers, his opponent leaves with a nails-up thrust to the chest. If the opponent does not counter it by the same edges with another nails-up thrust, and presses on it to his left side, the enemy frees with due speed and give a nails-down thrust into the chest. If the opponent undoes this thrust, pressing on it to his right side, one leaves with a high *tajo,* leaving the face guarded with the quillons. Additionally, if this is parried, leave with a *reves*, leaving the quillons covering the face in a manner that the enemy is not able to wound with any blow that he may throw.

Chapter Twenty-Three

The two established nails-up, one of them may gain the sword to the left side. If the opponent frees below, give him a nails-up thrust in the eyes without putting in the foot as he straightens to leave, extending only the sword arm. This thrust can be defended at the time that the opponent goes to gain the sword, but before he actually gains it: Leave by the point of the opponent's sword and give a *tajo* in the face by the edges of the same sword, entering suddenly at the same time. Take note that the right side remains uncovered, and that if the opponent leaves with a *reves* to the face, quickly turn nails-down from the wrist, leaving the sword outside of the face.

Chapter Twenty-Four

Established nails-up, at the time that the opponent lowers, the other commits a nails-up thrust. If the opponent presses on the sword in a
f.25 manner that the swords remain crossed, one of them turns the hand nails-up, bending the hand at the wrist (as well as it is), over the sword, and thrusts nails-up in the eyes, which can be given any time that one is crossed with a *tajo.* When this thrust is given, the opponent's shoulder remains uncovered. If the enemy loads with a nails-up thrust to said place, one may easily turn the sword nails-down, and it will be parried; at the same time he turns it, he should give a nails-down thrust in the face.

Chapter Twenty-Five

The two established nails-up, one of them gains the opponent's sword from below in a way that they remain crossed, and at the same time commits a *tajo* to the face. If the opponent goes to parry, he quickly turns with a nails-down thrust to the eyes. The opponent can defend himself as the opponent throws the *tajo* by retreating backwards, or retreating the foot, taking the *tajo* in the quillons, and giving a nails-up thrust in the eyes.

Chapter Twenty-Six

Being established nails-up, if the opponent throws a *reves*, while manipulating the hand in order to arm it, the opponent gives a nails-up thrust before the *reves* passes. If the enemy lowers with speed to beat said thrust, you free below to the outside and turn to give a nails-down thrust in the same place. The blow made, leave by cutting *tajo* and *reves.*

Chapter Twenty-Seven

Established like this, if the opponent throws said *reves* to the legs, and it passes before you defend it nails-up as said above, withdraw the foot so that the *reves* passes and give a nails-up thrust in the eyes. If the opponent rips it with a *tajo*, free the best that you are able and turn with the same nails-up thrust at the eyes, taking the parry in the quillons. Note that any time you make a similar parry, that it should be from the side, and that your head stays behind the quillons.

Chapter Twenty-Eight f.26

The two established, if one of them lowers a bit so that he uncovers only the breast, do not wait, but quickly attack the opponent with a nails-up thrust to the chest, leaving then with a *tajo* and *reves.*

Chapter Twenty-Nine

Established nails-up, one of them lifts the point of the sword in the air, leaving the quillons in front of the chest. If the opponent thrusts nails-up, lower quickly with a nails-up thrust by the same edges at the eyes. When the opponent defends said thrust by the edges, then if he presses the sword to the right side, leave by the point of his sword in the manner of a *reves* and, in arriving to his sword's point, turn quickly at the wrist, giving a nails-down thrust in the chest while entering with the left foot.

Chapter Thirty

The two established nails-up, when one of them lowers, the opponent thrusts nails-up to the eyes. This is defended by gaining the sword, entering suddenly, and at the same time giving a *reves* in the face, reaching well to the opponent. If one doesn't want to use this *reves*, wait so that the enemy leaves to free, and when he frees, give a nails-up thrust in the face before he straightens the sword.

Chapter Thirty-One

The two established nails-up, one of them passes the sword below the opponent's sword to the right side and ends nails-down. If the enemy commits a nails-up thrust to the chest, respond to it with a nails-down thrust to the same place, while putting in the left foot. If the opponent commits the said thrust nails-down and not nails-up, free below his sword and give him a nails-up thrust below the arm, then retreat while cutting with a long *tajo* and *reves.*

f.27

Chapter Thirty-Two

Established nails-up, as said in Chapter Thirty-One, when the opponent commits the thrust, free below and defend it by the same edges. Not wanting to do so, press the sword to his left side and give him a *tajo* in the face. If the opponent would be warned at the time you press, he may leave by the point with a *reves* to your face before you take control of his sword, entering suddenly.

Chapter Thirty-Three

leave from where the *reves* leaves

The two established, if one of them leaves with a *reves* to the legs, the opponent withdraws the leg and gives a *tajo* in the face with the wrist. One who would understand this art takes note that since the author said that one leaves with a *reves* from the nails-up posture, one must understand that the *reves* leaves from where it leaves, and the counter is made to it, not to the place it left.

Chapter Thirty-Four

the testing, since it has to be with consideration, it should be with courage

Established nails-up, if one of them tests[72] the opponent's sword, the opponent can leave by the point and give a *tajo* in the face by the same edges of the sword. Also when they go to test, he can give a *tajo* in the elbow from below, and go at the same time to the face with another *tajo*, circling closely around the hand and arm.

Chapter Thirty-Five

the sword should run the edges of the opponent's

The two established nails-up, if one of them makes a low nails-up posture with the point one palm[73] from the floor, the opponent is attacked with a nails-up thrust to the thigh, moving out of the way to the right side, with the left foot turning to the rear, and the thrust pressing the quillons to the left side in a manner that the enemy cannot attack nor meet the opponent's thigh. This can be defended by taking the foot back and giving a nails-up thrust in the face, or doing the same as the one who commits the thrust.

f.28

Chapter Thirty-Six

Established nails-up, the two swords being matched, you gain the opponent's sword in the middle third. Then, turn your sword's towards the point at the point of the opponent's sword, and turning your shoulders so that they remain on the opponent's sword, give a nails-down thrust in the eyes, gaining the quillons with the hand. Note that all these precautions that are made in order to give this have to be made at the same time.

Chapter Thirty-Seven

Established nails-up, test the opponent's sword. If he consents to you, commit a threatening nails-up thrust at the eyes. If the opponent only raises to defend it, lower quickly with a nails-up thrust below the arm, retreating backwards. If the enemy continues to you with a nails-up thrust, rip with a *tajo*, withdrawn low.

Chapter Thirty-Eight

The two established nails-up, one of them lowers his sword over his left foot and leg, remaining nails-up. If the opponent thrusts nails-up to the chest, he may quickly pass his sword to the opponent's left side, below his sword, and give a nails-up thrust by the same edges, or give a nails-down thrust in the chest without passing the sword — putting in the foot somewhat.

retreating the body

Chapter Thirty-Nine

The two being established nails-up, one of them opens nails-down at the same height. If the opponent commits a nails-up thrust to the chest, defend by the same edges. In place of giving said thrust by the same edges, one can also press on the sword, and if the opponent frees below, give him a nails-up thrust in the eyes while he frees. The same is done if he will leave by the point.

Chapter Forty

f.29

Being established nails-up, one of them may gain the opponent's sword from above, ending nails-down. If the enemy consents, he turns from the wrist to thrust nails-up at the eyes. When they gain the sword, the opponent will be able to free at the same time and give a nails-up thrust in the chest, not entering, but retreating.

Chapter Forty-One

This same thrust above, when the opponent frees the sword, a nails-down thrust can be given in the belly, bending to the left side, when it rises. If the enemy takes the foot and leg back and thrusts nails-up at the eyes, rip with a *tajo* that cuts from the left shoulder to the right knee, which the opponent can take in the quillons from nails-up, giving the same thrust to the eyes.

Chapter Forty-Two

The two armed nails-up, if you test the opponent's sword, and he consents to it, give a nails-up thrust to the eyes. If the opponent defends it nails-up by the same edges, quickly turn the hand nails-down and give the same thrust in the eyes, inclining the body to the left side. When he defends said thrust by the edges, you can also retreat only the body backward, remaining nails-up; when the enemy withdraws, press on it with the same nails-up thrust to the eyes.

Chapter Forty-Three

Established nails-up, if one of them lowers the sword, give a blow to the opponent's chest. If he presses on it with the nails up, take the sword with both hands on the quillons and give a nails-up thrust by the edges to the eyes, or give a *tajo* to the thigh, withdrawing when the blow falls.

f.30

Chapter Forty-Four

The two armed nails-up, one of them may threaten a nails-up thrust on the outside. If the opponent deflects it, threaten the same thrust to the inside. If the opponent turns to deflect it, return and give a nails-up thrust outside in the shoulder, which the opponent can defend with a nails-down thrust to the same shoulder.

Chapter Forty-Five

Armed nails-up, one of them may give a touch under the arm with the wrist, leaning back. If the opponent prepares a nails-up thrust, defend it with a nails-up thrust by the same edges or rip it with a *tajo* to the face. If the opponent retreats from the *tajo*, so it passes in vain, and returns to make a nails-up thrust, you should rip it with a *reves* to the legs. The opponent can defend this *reves* by giving a nails-down thrust in the thigh. This can be defended by taking back the foot and body, but note that it has to be with much speed.

Chapter Forty-Six

Both armed nails-up, threaten a nails-up thrust to the opponent. If the opponent does not defend it by pressing, or by the edges, but by only lifting, turn quickly when he lifts and give a nails-up thrust below the arm, then leave while cutting *tajo* and *reves*. The thrust below the arm is defended by quickly turning when he lifted and giving a nails-down thrust on the outside on the right side of the sword, entering somewhat with the body.

Chapter Forty-Seven

Established nails-up, one may touch under the arm, retreating back. If the opponent prepares a nails-up thrust to the eyes, enter suddenly, gaining the sword up to the middle, and then enter more with a *reves* to the face. Note that if you give this *reves* without entering, the opponent is able to wound you in the face. When you will go with the *reves*, gain the quillons with your hand. All one time

Chapter Forty-Eight f.31

The two armed nails-up, if one of them lowers the sword, the opponent can thrust nails-up. If the enemy defends the same thrust that you were going to give nails-up by the edges, give it nails-down instead, in the same place where the nails-up thrust was going without making a second movement, inclining the body to the left side.

The *diestro*[74] notes now – When this thrust is defended by the same edges, it is necessary that he gains the opponent's sword with his quillons, and when gained, one cannot stop the point from falling to the shoulder, where the joint of the bones go. So then, if it is necessary that the quillons are joined to the opponent's sword, when they come together, if the opponent is found nails-down, the sword cannot be joined without the point of it falling outside of that place where it would fall if he found it nails-up. As the opponent bends the body and turns the hand with the nails-down thrust, it is clear that the nails-down Note thrust in that place retains its value. One can use this thrust every time that he has to defend the nails-up thrust by the same edges.

Chapter Forty-Eight[75]

In Chapter Forty-two, we deal with a rule no worse than the others, but because it doesn't go declared and seems difficult and false, it is best that it is mentioned and related, as with the rule above.

It says in the rule that with the two armed nails-up, if one of them lowers, the opponent commits a nails-up thrust to the chest, and if it is defended by the same edges, the opponent retreats enough that it doesn't reach him with the step that is brought, remaining nails-up when he retreats. If the opponent continues the same thrust, defend it by the same edges, because this thrust that is contradicted by the
f.32 same edges cannot be reformed, except by the opponent retreating. The opponent cannot stop moving, seeing himself tricked, and with much more spirit than in the first, and it is such that the opponent who responds is the one who attacked before, and the attacker is the one who responded before. Although it is said that it cannot be reformed, if he retreats well when the opponent arrives, he can undo the thrust by the same edges, pressing on the sword in the middle third. If the opponent frees below, or by the point, give the nails-up thrust in the face as said before.

Chapter Forty-Nine

Being established nails-up, if the enemy gains your sword in the middle third, respond to it with a *reves* to the head. If the opponent parries such that the two end crossed, quickly turn the hand nails-up above the sword and give a nails-up thrust in the face. Note that
Or *reves*
if the opponent comes with a nails-up thrust to the shoulder that is uncovered, turn nails-down quickly and you will be free.

Chapter Fifty

The two established nails-up, one commits a nails-up thrust to the
If the sword remains in such height
quillons hand. If the opponent withdraws the hand backwards, press over it with a nails-up thrust to the eyes by the same edges. The opponent can defend the thrust to the hand by lowering his sword hand and giving a nails-down thrust in the belly at the same time, or lifting

said hand and giving a nails-down thrust in the chest. In this manner, when you give the nails-down thrust into the belly, the opponent's sword remains above in vain, and when you give the nails-down thrust in the chest, the opponent's sword remains below in vain. A *tajo* can be given in place of the thrust to the chest.

Chapter Fifty-One: How the Nails-Up Thrusts Leaving from the Testing Posture Are Given

Note that after testing the opponent's sword, thrusts to the chest have to gain the opponent's sword with the quillons in the manner f.33
of a thrust given by the same edges, because what use is it to me to test the opponent's sword if I leave it free when I thrust to the chest, leaving the same action for my enemy as for me? Having tested my opponent's sword, if I want to set off with a nails-up thrust to the chest, it has to be in the manner of gaining the sword with the quillons.

Chapter Fifty-Two

The two established, if one of them drills,[76] which is called by the name of *garatusa,* in effect scrawling[77] the opponent's sword, the opponent frees at the same time, giving the nails-up thrust in the chest. Or, when the *garatusa* begins, and the opponent's sword is above yours, press on your sword and give a nails-down thrust in the thigh, or free with a nails-down thrust to the chest.

Chapter Fifty-Three

After being established nails-up, if one of them opens nails-down, and the opponent thrusts nails-up to the chest, defend it with a nails-up thrust by the same edges. From the same posture, if the opponent lowers, thrust nails-up to the eyes, which can be defended from nails-up by the same edges. If the opponent presses it, leave with *reves* and *tajo*.

Chapter Fifty-Four

The two established nails-up, or in whichever posture that they may be, the opponent throws a *reves* to the legs. Run a nails-down or nails-up thrust to the inside of the thigh at the height in which the opponent parted. If the opponent leaves with a *reves* to the head, in the moment he manipulates the *reves*, raise and give a nails-down thrust into the chest. If he raises for a *tajo*, leave with a nails-up thrust to the eyes. If he leaves with a nails-up thrust, it is defended by the same edges nails-up, leaving quickly, cutting with *tajo* and *reves*. Note that this *reves* to the legs is bad to know; in its place it is revealed.

f.34

Chapter Fifty-Five

The two established nails-up, if you test the sword, and the opponent frees below, you can also free below behind it and run a nails-up thrust to the chest at the same time. Note that when you free, the sword should be as close to the opponent's as possible – This same thrust will be given when your sword passes nails-down to the opponent's right side. Being so, if attacked by a nails-up or nails-down thrust, leave below his and give a nails-up thrust in the chest.

Chapter Fifty-Six

The two established nails-up, if one of them lowers the sword and messes with it, moving it around, outside to inside and back again, quickly commit a nails-up thrust to the chest. This posture is one that the masters don't have to consent to as much as teach it. What does it serve to move the sword with flourishes while the opponent's sword is in his face?

Chapter Fifty-Seven

Established nails-up, one lowers. If the opponent lowers after it, the other raises to thrust nails-up to the chest, which can be defended by a nails-up thrust by the same edges. It can also be deflected with a *tajo*. When he leaves with the thrust to the chest, the opponent can retreat and give a touch under the arm at the same time, which is contradicted by turning the hand and arm nails-down, the arm ending with the elbow up, and giving a nails-down thrust in the chest. In place of this thrust, a *tajo* can be given in the face.

Chapter Fifty-Eight

Established nails-up in the lower posture, if the opponent starts off with a nails-up thrust to the thigh, withdraw the leg and give a nails-up thrust in the eyes. Since this rule was given before, another is dealt with here by bringing a different counter; the opponent can also give a blow of *tajo* in the crook of the elbow when he lowers, which can be given every time that the opponent will lower.

Chapter Fifty-Nine f.35

When the opponent commits a *tajo* or *reves* to the head from whichever posture that is in, a nails-up thrust can be given in the eyes when he lifts. If starting off with a *reves*, the nails-up thrust can be given in the eyes before the sword passes from the right side. This thrust can be defended by abandoning the blow and gaining the enemy's sword, taking note of the quickness that he must have, so that the opponent does not free the sword and give the same nails-up thrust as before.

Chapter Sixty

Established nails-up, being long (as much as you can be), if the opponent gives a *reves*, and you recognize that it goes to the lower parts, wait for it at the pass with a nails-up thrust from below in the armpit, with which you will give two wounds: This, and the sword arm going on your sword and cutting itself. Note that you have to give this thrust before the sword passes from the outside.

Chapter Sixty-One

Established nails-up or committing a nails-up thrust, if the opponent commits a blow to the elbow,[78] turn the arm in a circle, rotating the elbow upward as much as you can, and at the same time run a nails-down thrust to the chest. Also, when the opponent manipulates the hand in order to give said blow, wait for it with a nails-up thrust below the chest from the right side.

Chapter Sixty-Two

The two established nails-up, when the opponent tests your sword, free below and pass your sword to the outside. If the opponent turns to test it from that side where you have armed yourself, turn quickly below to free it, ending on the inside where it was before, and give a nails-up thrust by the edges. Note that freeing and giving the thrust is all one.

f.36

Chapter Sixty-Three

Being established nails-up, when the opponent passes the sword below the enemy's to the outside, one can also give a blow of *tajo* in the crook of the elbow, retreating. If the opponent continues with a nails-up thrust, deflect it with a *tajo* or give a nails-up thrust by the same edges.

Chapter 65 does this, and Chapter 71 the same, and Chapter 4, 132

attacking freeing and simple freeing

Chapter Sixty-Four: What Is Freeing

Because freeing the sword is dealt with many times in these rules, I advise that freeing is nothing other than escaping the weapon of the enemy, who intends to gain it with his so that he commits the blow more safely. By that, he who will profess this art in no case has to consent that the enemy may be lord of it, testing it with his, nor gaining it in the middle third, but escaping and putting it where it suits him before it may be captive, except when one wants to consent in order to trick him.

Chapter Sixty-Five

Established nails-up, test the opponent's sword, and if he frees nails-up to the eyes, defend it nails-down to the chest. The opponent can undo this nails-down thrust, freeing below, giving a nails-up thrust by the edges in the eyes.

freeing

He that has to free notes that when freeing, as dealt with in Chapter 64, he has to be armed together with retreating the body backwards when he frees, so that the opponent doesn't give a nails-up thrust in the face or a blow to the head, which will not be necessary when freeing from afar.

Chapter Sixty-Six

The two established nails-up, the opponent attacks with a nails-up thrust to the eyes. If the enemy lifts, not defending nails-up by the edges or another offensive counter, lower the same thrust and give it close to the armpit, lifting the quillons nails-up, keeping the head covered behind them.

Chapter Sixty-Seven

f.37

The two established nails-up, you gain the opponent's sword in the middle third entering suddenly. As soon as it is gained, give a *reves* in the face while entering forward with another step. If the opponent leaves with a *tajo*, you will remain free, turning the sword nails-up, leaving with *reves* and *tajo*, the quillons remaining always in front of the face.

Chapter Sixty-Eight: Testing The Opponent's Sword

Every time that you test the opponent's sword after being armed nails-up, take care that the opponent does not leave below, giving a blow in the leg. If he does, continue with a nails-up thrust below the chest, so that he cannot give a *balanzada.* You will keep to the same advice every time that you gain said sword, and when you test the opponent's sword, it should be swaying the body back.

Chapter Sixty-Nine

Established nails-up, if the opponent commits a nails-down thrust to the eyes, it cannot be defended with a nails-up thrust without the left foot and body turning toward the rear, in the manner that Chapter 84 ahead deals with the nails-up thrust with the wheeling step,[79] because in not turning the body back, although he gives the thrust, he will not stop the opponent from giving it from nails-down, because of the circle that the arm makes when armed nails-down.

Chapter Seventy

Established nails-up, one of them tests the opponent's sword in almost the middle third, or perhaps on the point. If the opponent neglects to free, give a *reves* in the face without putting in the foot, or any more than extending the sword hand and arm. The opponent can defend it by the same edges. I mean to say, by withdrawing the head so that the *reves* passes in vain and giving a nails-up thrust in the eyes, which can be defended by a nails-up thrust by the same edges.

f.38

Chapter Seventy-One: Freeing

this chapter has to be joined to Chapter 88, which has one more technique[80] than this

The two armed nails-up very close, with the points of the swords in the air, the opponent can step the right foot back, letting the sword fall to nails-up. If the opponent retreats, follow him with the same nails-up thrust, returning to put in the foot that you had taken back. From this same posture, you can withdraw the hand with the wrist in a manner that the sword that he had on the inside ends outside, and if it will be on the outside, it ends on the inside. Done how I say with the wrist, it will be freed with more speed than if you do it with arm, which doesn't free with as much speed.

The chest

Attacking Freeing

All the manners of freeing (as touched on in Chapters 65 and 64) don't have to be withdrawing the hand toward the rear, but moving with the wrist. As well, if the enemy gains your sword, when you free you won't withdraw the arm toward the rear, into which the opponent will attack with a nails-up thrust, but give an air to the wrist and then go below the opponent's sword until it leaves close to the quillons, and execute your blow.

Chapter Seventy-Two

The two established nails-up, if they will come together such that without putting in foot or body, the sword can reach the opponent's face, turn the hand nails-down and give a touch in the face with the wrist, returning quickly to the same posture that you were in before. If the opponent presses on your sword to the outside, turn from the wrist by the point of the opponent's sword and give a nails-down thrust in the chest.

Chapter Seventy-Three

The two established nails-up, if one of them tests the sword, you will be able to free for a nails-up thrust to the chest. Since it said before that it has to be nails-down, it's understood that the nails-down can free before he tests and after being tested, but the nails-up has to be before the sword has tested, being given before the sword arrives to the opponent's.

consent to this

Chapter Seventy-Four

Established nails-up, if the opponent tests the sword, consent to it. If the opponent thrusts nails-up to the eyes, retreat from this thrust so that he doesn't reach with it. If the opponent continues the same thrust, the opponent can defend it by the same edges nails-up thrust to the eyes, or turning nails-down, giving it in the same place. It's not the same as before, because this manner of retreat in this place is a technique[81] in itself.

Chapter Seventy-Five

Established nails-up, if the opponent throws a *reves*, respond to it with another. If the opponent continues the ripped *reveses*, when your sword goes above your head, turn from the wrist to thrust nails-up to the eyes. You will do the same when you play a *reves* against the opponent – if the opponent withdraws backward so that your sword passes in vain, turn from the wrist to thrust nails-up to the eyes. You will be able to do it quickly.

Chapter Seventy-Six

Established nails-up, when the opponent throws a *reves*, if the enemy gives a blow in the elbow, turn the hand nails-up from the wrist, lifting the arm to the eyes. If you are established nails-up low, and they commit a nails-up thrust to the thigh, deflect it to the outside and guard the face with *tajo* and *reves*.

Understand this *tajo* and *reves* well. One has to give it to he who commits a thrust to the thigh. If deflected, you can give the same *tajo* and *reves*.

Chapter Seventy-Seven

Established nails-up, if the opponent throws a *reves*, retreat back so that his sword passes in vain, and in passing, commit a nails-up thrust. When the enemy withdraws, the opponent can turn the *reves* that is going to the head, in order to descend and give a nails-up thrust in the chest.

Chapter Seventy-Eight

Established nails-up, if the opponent tests, leave with a nails-up thrust to the right shoulder on the outside when he comes to test.

Note this counter

The opponent can defend by giving the same nails-up thrust in the same place, dodging suddenly to the left side as quickly as possible.

f.40

Chapter Seventy-Nine: Blows Originating from the Nails-Down Posture

The two established nails-down, if one of them tests the sword, during time that it spends on arriving to said sword, the opponent gives a *reves* that cuts from the right shoulder to the left knee, retreating with it. This is defended by withdrawing the leg as much as necessary so that the *reves* passes, and continuing to the opponent with a nails-up thrust.

The moment he goes making the gaining

If the enemy defends this thrust by pressing on it, the opponent leaves with a *tajo*, freeing by the point of the enemy's sword. When this *tajo* is given, it has to enter suddenly, coming to the enemy such that the point of the sword remains behind, so that he doesn't give a thrust below.

How to Give the *Tajo* Leaving by the Point of the Opponent's Sword

Every time this *tajo* is given, it has to be in this form. If the enemy leaves with a *reves* to the right shoulder that remains uncovered, quickly turn nails-down and continue with the same nails-down thrust to the face. This *tajo* can be defended by giving a *balanzada*.

Chapter Eighty: How the Nails-Down Thrusts are Given with the Left Foot Put In – And How to Give Them

As we deal with the nails-down posture, it suits us to declare whether they will be safer putting in either the right or left foot. This does not excuse putting in one or the other, because the nails-down thrusts don't reach as far, because of the arm going in a circle, as those of nails-up, which necessarily have to be given with the arm extended. Not being given like this would be faulty in my opinion, except in better judgment.

Because the arm guards the body

I say that the nails-down thrusts have to be given putting in the left foot, because in putting in the left foot, he uncovers more of the opponent's chest and remains more distant from the opponent. Putting in the right foot leaves the opponent's chest more concealed, and the opponent will be defended with little diligence. The reason that some masters give, that taking the foot back at the time that the opponent puts his in, he will be given a thrust in the eyes, is not good. However, the foot should not be put in after the enemy tests or gains.

Chapter Eighty-One: More on the Previous Chapter

f.41

The two established, if one of them comes to test (and note that it says if he *comes to test*, not *after testing*, because putting in the foot with the thrust after testing has no place), then when the opponent comes to test the sword, put the left foot in and give a nails-down thrust in the chest. If the enemy leaves with the foot back thrusting nails-up to the chest, defend it with a nails-up thrust by the same edges. If he leaves with a *reves* to the legs, guard the leg and give the same nails-up thrust.

This nails-down thrust can also be defended when the foot is put in, by the opponent also putting in the left foot. When one puts the foot in, it should not be straight to the enemy, but to one side, and with the same nails-down thrust in the chest. *Note*

Chapter Eighty-Two

Established nails-down, if the opponent tests the sword, thrust nails-up before it arrives, gaining his sword in the quillons. If the enemy presses on your sword, leave with a *reves* and then respond with a *tajo*, not forgetting that the quillons will remain guarding the face and head, and not giving the blows in a manner that the quillons forsake the face.

Chapter Eighty-Three

The two established nails-down, when the opponent tests, a nails-down thrust can be given in the belly below his sword while putting in the foot. If the opponent leaves with a *tajo*, continue into a nails-up thrust, taking the blow in the quillons, but if the opponent leaves with a nails-up thrust to the shoulder on the outside when they test the sword, defend it with a nails-down thrust at the same height where the opponent's was coming, without putting in the foot.

If said thrusts do not reach execution, and the swords remain crossed, one of them may turn the hand nails-up from the wrist and give said

Not putting in the body

nails-up thrust in the eyes. If the opponent threatens the eyes with a nails-up thrust, turn to thrust nails-down to the same place.

f.42

Chapter Eighty-Four

Being established nails-down, give a nails-up thrust, rounding the left foot behind — elsewhere called a *wheeling step* — in a manner that you end with your back almost turned to the opponent. The opponent must do the same to free from said thrust. Before you thrust with the wheeling step, if he tests your sword, leave by the point of his sword with a *tajo* to the face.

Chapter Eighty-Five

Established nails-down, when the opponent tests the sword, free below and give a *tajo* in the face with the wrist, entering suddenly to your left side. Note that this *tajo* seems difficult, but it is not. Also, at the time that one frees, he will be able to give blow in the elbow when the sword leaves. This *tajo* is defended with a parry, responding with another.

Chapter Eighty-Six

Armed nails-down, if the opponent tests, run a *tajo* to the elbow when it goes. If the opponent lowers the sword, however little it may be, turn with a rounded *tajo* like in Chapter 85. This *tajo* can be defended in a different manner than before, because when he goes to give the elbow strike,[82] by turning nails-down, a thrust can be given nails-down in the chest, or when he goes to arm the wrist, give the nails-up thrust that had begun before.

Chapter Eighty-seven

The two armed nails-down, if one of them tests the sword, the opponent will commit a nails-up thrust to the quillons hand when he tests. If the enemy withdraws the arm at the time that said thrust is committed, the opponent continues with said thrust to the chest with nails-up, which can be defended by a nails-up thrust by the same edges. This same thrust that goes to the hand can be committed before the opponent tests, being armed nails-down.

Chapter Eighty-Eight: How This Chapter Is Dealt with in Chapter Seventy-One f.43

In Chapter Seventy-One we deal with the posture of the two crossed very close nails-up, which can be used in the same posture of nails-down, coming to cross close, in a manner that the same order that one finds it dealt with can be used in the nails-down posture, being crossed close as I say. One can add that when they are crossed, the sword arm can descend with a *tajo* to the shins, moving back from the opponent at the same time. If the opponent returns with a *reves*, lift the sword and take the parry.

Chapter Eighty-Nine

The two established nails-down, if one of them tests the opponent's sword, gain it from below in a manner that they remain crossed. In that same time, the opponent turns nails-up above his sword and gives a nails-up thrust in the eyes and then leaves, cutting with *tajo* and *reves* before the opponent commits a nails-up thrust.

Chapter Ninety

The two established nails-down, if one of them tests the opponent's sword, the opponent may free by the point of his sword and give a *tajo* in the face. The same can be done if the enemy gains it. Take note that when the opponent leaves, he may abandon the testing or gaining that he was making, and give a nails-up thrust in the eyes. Thus, it is very important that those that will test have care in the freeing and counters that originate from these movements.

Chapter Ninety-One

Above all, each one must be established first. Being established nails-down in that time that the opponent comes to establish is a great advantage, and you will commit a nails-up thrust to the chest. This thrust can be given while being established nails-up when the opponent comes to establish himself. When you give it, if they press to your right side, give a nails-down thrust in the chest, freeing quickly.

f.44

Chapter Ninety-Two

The two established nails-down, one commits a nails-up thrust to the eyes, not putting in the foot. If the opponent lifts without offense, lower the same nails-up thrust below the arm. If the opponent retreats with a *reves*, parry, responding with a *tajo* and another *reves*. Being established, if he tests you, put in the foot with a nails-down thrust to the chest, freeing below, which can be defended by also putting the left foot in and giving the same nails-down thrust in the same place, as already dealt with in another chapter.

Chapter Ninety-Three

Established nails-down, if the opponent tests, give a touch under the arm or a blow in the knee when he tests, the body inclined to the left side. If the opponent withdraws the foot with a nails-up thrust, you will be able to defend said thrust by ripping with a *tajo* or with a *reves*, or going by the same edges, gaining the sword in the quillons.

Chapter Ninety-Four

Established nails-down, when one tests the sword, the opponent comes with a *reves* to the head. At the time that the *reves* passes, give a blow of *reves* in the sword arm, retreating backwards. If the opponent continues with a nails-up thrust, lift, gaining the sword in the middle third, pressing to his left side. If he frees below, before he frees, in manipulating the hand, you will give a nails-up thrust in the eyes.

Chapter Ninety-Five

Being established nails-down, when the opponent tests you, leave with a *reves* to the head. Take note that one can put in the left foot and give a nails-down thrust in the face, to which you can leave with foot and body toward the rear, freeing the sword below his, and give a nails-up thrust in the eyes. If the opponent presses when one gives said thrust, give the same nails-down thrust below his sword, in the belly.

f.45

Chapter Ninety-Six

The two established nails-down, if the opponent starts off with a nails-up thrust to the chest, deviate the body to your left side so that his sword stays around the crook of the elbow of your right arm and give a nails-down thrust in the eyes or in the belly. When you commit the thrust to the eyes, if the opponent presses on the sword to your right side, then one can give the thrust in the belly and be safer. You will do the same if the opponent tests and gives a nails-up thrust to the chest or gives the same nails-up thrust by the same edges.

Chapter Ninety-Seven

Established nails-down, if the opponent tests your sword, gain it from below so that you remain crossed the most extended that you are able. If the enemy descends with a *reves* to the legs as many do, guard the leg where the blow goes and give a *tajo* or *reves* in thc hcad or a nails-up thrust in the eyes.

Chapter Ninety-Eight

Established nails-down, or in whichever posture that you play a high *tajo*, not so that the *tajo* is executed, as so that the opponent parries in a manner that they remain crossed. Turn at the wrist with a nails-down thrust to the belly, keeping your sword as close to the opponent's quillons as it can, and yours the highest that you can. When you give said thrust, enter a little forward.

Chapter Ninety-Nine

Established nails-up, if the opponent presses on your sword in a manner leaving the *reves* armed, you will suddenly give a jump with the left foot with much speed, leaving with a *reves* in the air, turning nails-down, and give said nails-down thrust in the face. Note that you don't enter close to the opponent, but to the side, so that it will be well-armed.

Chapter One-Hundred: On Four Techniques[83] and Blows with Which One Can Attack the Armored, Which Can Become Five or More f.46

All the people that will enter in a fight or quarrel have to take note that they have an obligation to experience the primary blows if the opponent is armored. When it is known, the opponent may test the sword, and if he consents to it, commit a nails-up thrust to the face, where the hidden armor never reaches. Even if the enemy doesn't consent, you will be so quick that it is barely tested when said thrust departs. When one will not go the way of testing, in the opponent removing the sword from in front of the face, whether by any lowering, any rising, or any opening, commit said thrust with speed.

Chapter One-Hundred One

Seeing the opponent armored, one can also attack him when established with a nails-up thrust to the sword hand in front of the quillons, as well as when the weapon cuts with *tajo* or *reves*, taking note that when he cuts with a *tajo*, said thrust has to be committed nails-up, because missing the thrust, it is parried — and when he cuts with a *reves*, commit said thrust nails-down, because in this way, missing said thrust, it is parried.

Chapter One-Hundred Two

The armored man can be attacked in the armpit where the armor does not reach. When the armored one manipulates the hand to arm a *tajo*, commit a nails-up thrust to said armpit, or press on the sword to his right side so that he leaves with a *reves* (which is easy for armored people to commit), in beginning to manipulate the *reves*, give him said nails-up thrust in the armpit.

Note — Take note in all that your sword doesn't go flourishing with *tajos* or *reveses*, which have no place against the armored, but established nails-up at the eyes and freeing in all occasions.

f.47

Chapter One-Hundred Three

One can also give a nails-up or nails-down thrust in the thigh from the inside.[84] When the armored arms with a low nails-up posture, run the nails-up thrust, gaining his sword with the quillons of yours. However, the better technique[85] is that you press on his sword so that he leaves with a *reves* to your lower parts. When the *reves* passes, run the thrust nails-down to the left thigh, running the thrust inside. If you do not have time for any of this, threaten said armored opponent with a nails-up thrust to the eyes, and in lifting or defending it by the same edges, give him a *balanzada* nails-down thrust to the thighs, and then lift it so his counter doesn't arrive.

Chapter One-Hundred Four

This same rule can be used if the two come with double weapons, but if the opponent is found with sword and dagger, against the armored he takes all the blows on the sword and enters to give the blows with the dagger.

Chapter One-Hundred Five

Armed nails-down, if perhaps you have been mistreated by the opponent, it seems good to retreat by stepping, and you risk losing your sword, give a nails-up throwing thrust[86] to the chest. When you give it armed nails-down like this, withdraw the arm toward the rear so that the force takes air, and turning the hand nails-up, throw the sword to the chest. If you want to experience this thrust, throw it at a wall with a practice sword, and you will see the force that it brings, which you will be able to give to the opponent. Note

Chapter One-Hundred Six: Two Wounds in One Time

Established nails-down, or in whichever manner that one may be when the opponent throws a *reves* to the legs, defend it with a nails-down thrust given below the breast. If the opponent lifts with a *reves*, give the same thrust above in the chest. If he lifts with a *tajo*, give a nails-up thrust in the eyes.

Chapter One-Hundred Seven: Deals with the *Balanzada* Thrusts Being Good, which Are Misunderstood By Many f.48

I have found myself in certain places and provinces where someone talking about this art wanted to praise some person as a *diestro*. If I ask them whether that person whom they were praising knew the *balanzadas*, and they answer no, then, he's not a *diestro*, nor half a *diestro*. They gave the reason that those that play the *balanzadas* are very adept[87] in the weapons. One cannot be a *diestro*, however much he knows, without being adept. Then, if he had been adept, he would have known the *balanzadas*. If he doesn't know them, he is not adept. If he is not adept, he is not a *diestro*. Although one can respond to me that one can be adept in all the rest of the play, though not in the *balanzadas*; to that, I respond that in this way he will be a *player*, but not a *diestro*. A *diestro* understands how to play the art completely, not only meaning with all weapons, but completely skilled[88] in one weapon, or in another, or another, in order to teach enough to know it, and to teach to make one adept. In contrast, he that plays is not.

Chapter One-Hundred Eight: How to Understand the *Balanzadas*

I certainly believe (if I am not mistaken) that the rules of the *balanzadas* will be accepted by all, as they are by famous players that have experienced them, and by masters no less skilled in them than the *diestros*. If he that presumes to be a *diestro* approves of them (as dealt with in the chapter before), they don't ignore them. If they are ignored, they commit them out of place. The reader (and he that presumes to understand the art) should note that the *balanzada* thrust has to be given not in attack, but in response, because if they are given in attacking time, they run into danger, because the opponent responds and catches him in the act. Even though they are given safely many times in this manner, others are met with the counter. Being given in responding time as will be seen ahead, they will understand the safety of them and won't say that they can be committed falsely, as there is a place for the tricks.

Chapter One-Hundred Nine: How to Start Off the *Balanzada* Thrusts

Established in whatever posture that he will be, one of the two lowers his sword, retreating the body back, leaving the right foot in the place where it was when he lowered and retreated only with the left, loading on it. If the opponent departs with a nails-up thrust to the eyes or chest, as soon as he departs, incline yourself to your left side, not putting the eyes on the ground, but on the opponent's sword, and thrust nails-down to the belly. You will pass to the other side of the opponent. Start off all the *balanzada* thrusts in this manner, going at the time that the opponent attacks. For this, the farther you arm yourself from the opponent, the more securely you will be able to give it, because in order to reach, the opponent attacks with more force, and in departing, he will not be able to reform in the air, in a manner that when the *balanzada* thrust reaches execution, the opponent arrives with his thrust to that place that was left by he who did the *balanzada*. He cannot turn to respond without easily being responded to with a parry.

If this *balanzada* thrust was given (outside of firm to firm), it is easy to give the counter in such place with the foot taken back, which is impossible to do after he departs, and the counters that are given to such are pointed out in their place. f.49 Note

Chapter One-Hundred Ten

The two established, one may lower his sword (as before) to retreat. If the opponent commits a nails-up thrust, the other retreats when he commits it, and when the opponent returns to attack a second time, he gives a *balanzada* in the manner of Chapter 109. Being established nails-up, one of the two may also give a blow with the wrist below the arm, close to the opponent's quillons, and at the same time retreat as f.50
much as he will be able. If the opponent thrusts nails-up, give a nails-down *balanzada* thrust to the belly in said manner.

Counter of Parry
Take note that when these thrusts are given with a practice sword, all the times after having given the blow, and not before, the opponent can turn with a *reves* behind, so when you give said blow, take the parry by lifting the sword with the point in the air.

Chapter One-Hundred Eleven

The two established nails-up, lower the sword in said manner. If the opponent doesn't lower or attack, lift with a nails-up thrust to the eyes with the spirit of executing it, which you will do if the enemy doesn't respond with the remedy – but if he lifts or goes by the same edges, give a *balanzada* in said mode. Being established, you can commit a *tajo* to the opponent's foot, retreating as has been dealt with. If the opponent gives a nails-up thrust, give a *balanzada* in said manner, and take note of the speed that is required.

Chapter One-Hundred Twelve

Established nails-up or nails-down, if the opponent tests your sword, consent, and if he thrusts nails-up to the eyes from that posture, give a *balanzada* as has been said. After being established, you can also play a false, lost *tajo* that passes in vain without encountering your opponent or his weapon. If the opponent commits a nails-up thrust after the *tajo* passes, give a *balanzada* in said manner. Note that when you play the *tajo*, you retreat because of the danger of the nails-up thrust to the eyes that the opponent can commit, and in committing it, you can also give a *balanzada* at the same time.

Chapter One-Hundred Thirteen

A lost *reves* can be thrown in the same manner, and if the opponent thrusts when the *reves* passes in vain, give a *balanzada.* Also, when you play the above *tajo*, if the opponent will only go to the nails-up parry without committing a thrust, give a *balanzada* in said manner.

f.51 **Chapter One-Hundred Fourteen**

Established nails-up, if you test the opponent's sword, and he leaves by the point of the sword with a *tajo* to your head, give a *balanzada* — the same if he will be armed nails-down. Mention of this *tajo* was made before, and in Chapter 129 also; where one can be sure of it, it is not a *tajo* that cuts from high to low, but to the right. When pressing on the opponent's sword to his left side, the same *balanzada* thrust will be able to be given if he will leave by the point with a *reves*, in the manner that the *tajo* leaves, as will be seen in Chapter 129.

Chapter One-Hundred Fifteen

Established nails-up, lower the sword, leaning as was said before. If the opponent commits a nails-up thrust, rip it with a *tajo.* If he parries nails-up, give a *balanzada* in said manner. You will do the same, being established high nails-up, gaining the opponent's sword above, not beating it down, because the higher the better. If the opponent frees, give a *balanzada* before he frees, in the manner already said.

Chapter One-Hundred Sixteen

Established nails-up, test the opponent's sword. If the opponent frees, committing a nails-down thrust to the chest, give a *balanzada;* you will do the same if he goes nails-up. Being established nails-down, if the opponent commits a nails-up thrust to the chest, give a *balanzada.* You will do the same, being established nails-down, when you test the opponent's sword. Testing it, if the opponent thrusts nails-up at the eyes by the same edges when it begins, give a *balanzada* as it is said.

Chapter One-Hundred Seventeen

Established nails-up, the opponent commits a nails-down thrust at the eyes. If it is defended nails-up, swaying the body and turning the left foot back, he who committed the first nails-down thrust can give a *balanzada* in said manner when the enemy defends with said nails-up thrust. The same can be done when established nails-up, if the opponent commits said nails-down thrust as was said: Not defending nails-up, one can give a *balanzada* in said manner. f.52

Chapter One-Hundred Eighteen

Established nails-up, if the opponent tests or presses on the sword, leave with a *tajo* from the wrist.

If the opponent gives the crossing parry, take the sword with both hands and thrust to the belly. One can also do this with the head put very low. Note

Chapter One-Hundred Nineteen

Established in whatever manner that it may be that the opponent attacks with a *reves*, take note that if you are armed nails-up at that time with the point at the eyes, don't take the point of the sword from where it is, so that when the *reves* goes circling, the same thrust is given in the face. To this, a *balanzada* can be given. Note this thrust

Chapter One-Hundred Twenty: How the *Reves* Is Less Dangerous Played from Firm to Firm, Armed Nails-Up, than from Any Other Time

This is not placed

One blindness going among the *diestros* is that the *reves* played from firm to firm is dangerous. I say that it is not dangerous, but safer, because the danger that the *reves* has is that when the opponent is armed in order to give it, the enemy can easily give a nails-up thrust in the eyes or chest. So I question whether this thrust will go safer when the opponent gains your sword and presses well on your right side, leaving from there with a *reves* being open, or whether from edge to edge, the swords nails-up. I say that the thrust is safer when the *reves* leaves from the open time, because as soon as one manipulates, the same thrust goes to the face at that time; being closed, the *reves* is given with the wrist, and the quillons always go in front of the face.

Chapter One-Hundred Twenty-One: Response Is One Thing, Counter Is Another

So that you are disillusioned, understand that when they give a blow, and you give another, that can't be called a counter, but a response, because a counter is avoiding the blow that comes to injure me, and at the same time injuring the opponent.

f.53 **Chapter One-Hundred Twenty-Two: The Counters to the *Balanzadas*, without Form or Order**

When the opponent gives a *balanzada*, turn the left foot and body back and wait for the opponent and thrust nails-up at the eyes, or do the same with a nails-down thrust, or do the same, waiting with a *tajo* to the head, or gain the sword, deflecting it to his right side when he gives a *balanzada*, and give the same *tajo* in the face – but the best in my opinion is a *reves*, because the thrusts and the *tajo*, as they are directed to the part where the opponent gives a *balanzada*, his speed can be so much that he passes without the counters getting in the way, but the *reves* arrives at its end where he who gives the *balanzada* comes to his. Thus, if he is not found in the entry, he is found in the end, because the *reves* is given circling all the body behind he who gives the *balanzada*. The reason why the body is taken back with the foot is because the opponent puts in the step with his foot.

Chapter One-Hundred Twenty-Three: Deals with Tricks

Whenever committing whichever technique[89] he thinks of, one cannot truly be a diestro without being able to commit whichever technique he thinks of, and when the opponent defends falsely so that his blow is undone, suddenly executing his strike, no more or less than committing the blow falsely. Note that the opponent also attacks falsely, so that with this advice, they will always be advised of the remedy: A trick is committing a *tajo* and leaving with a *reves*, committing a *reves* and leaving with a *tajo*, committing a thrust at the eyes and giving a *balanzada* or *baqueada*,[90] committing a thrust and leaving with a *tajo* or with a *reves*, testing so that he frees carelessly and giving a *balanzada*.

Tricks are all those blows that are not given to where they are committed in the first instance. A trick is when you play a *tajo* so that the opponent leaves with a *reves*. A trick is when you throw a *tajo*, and the opponent withdraws the body so that it passes in vain and attacks you uncovered. A trick is after being armed in a closed posture, opening oneself to the opponent.

Chapter One-Hundred Twenty-Four: *Manoplados* f.54

Manoplados are what we call undoing the thrusts that the opponent commits, beating them with the left hand to one side or the other — like being established nails-down or nails-up, if the opponent commits a nails-up thrust, beat it with the hand to the floor and give a nails-down thrust in the chest, or a *reves* in the face, or a *tajo*, whichever suits best.

Chapter One-Hundred Twenty-Five

Being established nails-up, test the opponent's sword. If he leaves, give a *manoplado* to the left side and a nails-down thrust in the belly, or a *tajo*, or a *reves* at the leaving. You will be able to do the same when the opponent tests the sword. Consent, and if he leaves to thrust to the eyes, give a *manoplado* to one side or the other and give the thrust which would suit better, or *tajo*, or *reves*. They can do the same from the nails-down posture. The nails-up thrusts will be given when you will give a *manoplado* over your left arm, and the nails-down thrust, putting in the foot, when you will give a *manoplado* over your right arm.

The counter of the *manoplado* play is to give a *manoplado* also, but one should not consent to *brazal*. counters

Chapter One-Hundred Twenty-Six: About *Tajos* and *Reveses*, and Blows Originating from Them step

Every time the opponent is armed nails-up with the sword arm withdrawn, a *tajo* below the arm is possible, retreating toward the rear – the same as whenever the two are crossed (whether nails-up or nails-down), a *tajo* will be given in the shins,[91] going backwards from the opponent, lifting then the sword in order to take the opponent's blow, which is a *reves*. One can also, in this same time, give a *reves* in the same place, such that in lowering the sword to said *reves*, one gains the quillons of the opponent's sword with the hand from the inside, twisting them to the outside.

Chapter One-Hundred Twenty-Seven

If being established in whatever manner, the opponent takes the parry
f.55 in the quillons, giving a nails-up thrust in the face. Take note that one should not wait for the *tajo* to lower, but in lifting. Commit the thrust in a manner that doesn't leave the arm withdrawn — one can also stop giving said thrust and retreat backwards, so that the *tajo* passes in vain, and commit it in passing, but he who goes playing said *tajo*, as it happens that the opponent goes retreating with the body and lowering the sword so that the *tajo* passes in vain, instead of descending with a *tajo*, turn at the wrist and thrust nails-up to the chest.

Chapter One-Hundred Twenty-Eight

Crossed nails-down, give a *tajo* in the face. If the opponent parries, return with a ripped *reves*, retreating with it, or it is possible to give this *tajo* and then *reves* without leaving, but they have to be only with the wrist, the quillons going always in front of the face because of the parries. In this form they remain in the same cause that these blows are committed, the quillons always have to cover the face, with the *tajo* as well as with the *reves*. In the same way, you will play a *tajo* that cuts from the left shoulder to the right knee, and if the opponent gives the crossing parry, leave with another *tajo* below, from the knee to the head (I like this very much). If you come to cross near, leave with a *tajo* to the head, gaining the opponent's quillons with the hand — or being crossed, you can lower a bit, retreating, and if the opponent lowers, return to thrust nails-down to the chest.

Chapter One-Hundred Twenty-Nine

Arming whichever way that one may, if the opponent presses your sword to the right side, leave by the point of the opponent's sword with a *tajo*, and run your sword along the edges of his right to the face, not lifting the sword. If pressed to the left side, leave with a *reves* in the
f.56 same manner, always entering to the opponent suddenly when giving said blows. The counters of these blows already go in their place; because of that, they are not dealt with here.

Chapter One-Hundred Thirty

Whenever you come to cross nails-up, you can give a *reves* in the sword arm with the wrist, remaining with the quillons in front of the face. Whenever the opponent will come playing a long *tajo*, you can give a *tajo* from the wrist in the crook of the elbow. Whenever the opponent plays a long *reves*, you can give a *reves* in the arm.

Chapter One-Hundred Thirty-One

Established nails-up, if the opponent puts the leg in, give it a *tajo*, retreating. The same if the two are crossed together nails-down or nails-up: Leave cutting all the body. Although this technique[92] is very dangerous because of leaving from so close to the opponent, speed overcomes it.

Chapter One-Hundred Thirty-One[93]

The two established nails-up, if the opponent gains your sword from the inside to the outside, arming a *reves*, give a jump forward with the left foot with great speed so that you fall well in front of his right shoulder, not straight to him, but to a side, and give a *reves* in the nape of the neck[94] or give the *reves* in the back. Note that this *reves* is curious and is given many times.

Chapter One-Hundred Thirty-Two

Being in a safe posture, throw a *tajo*. If the opponent parries nails-up crossed, leave with the same *tajo*, cutting the arm that remains uncovered. Being established nails-down, if the opponent tests your sword, when he starts off, you will be able to give a *tajo* in the legs, loading to the left side. If the opponent responds with a *reves*, lift quickly, parrying, and having parried, leave giving a *reves* in the legs, and note that you go uncovered.

Chapter One-Hundred Thirty-Three f.57

Being established nails-up, if the opponent gains your sword, leave below his with the wrist and turn with a *tajo* to the face, circling the arm, and note this *tajo* well. You will be able to give this same *tajo* when the opponent gains the sword up to the thirds, freeing quickly below with the wrist and giving a rounded *tajo* in the face. Note that you cannot free the sword without lifting the right foot such that it passes, then returning to set it down, making whichever air backwards with the body so that the sword passes freely. When the sword leaves, you can give a blow in the opponent's leg, and much speed is required for it.

Chapter One-Hundred Thirty-Four

Established nails-up or nails-down with the points to the floor, gain the opponent's sword on the inside and give a *reves* in the leg. You can also give a *reves* in place of a *tajo* in the form of Chapter 138. Note that when you free the sword as it mentions, it has to be with the point to the floor.[95]

Chapter One-Hundred Thirty-Five

The two established nails-up, or in whatever manner that the opponent goes to beat away[96] your sword. Before his sword reaches yours, give a *tajo* to the face in a manner that you go ahead of his sword, and when the opponent arrives, you have given the *tajo*, which has no place if the opponent met your sword when he went to beat it away. Whenever the opponent throws a *tajo* to the legs, take only the low crossed parry, and when the blow arrives, leave by the point of his sword with a *reves* to the face, reaching the opponent all in an instant.

f.58 ### Chapter One-Hundred Thirty-Six

The two established nails-up, if the opponent commits a nails-up thrust to the eyes or chest and brings the arm withdrawn, commit a *tajo* to the elbow, and at the same time circle to the face, which can be freed, being parried. Established nails-up, pass the sword to the outside of the opponent, and if he commits a thrust to where it is, rip with a *reves*.

Chapter One-Hundred Thirty-Seven

Established in whichever manner that it may be that the opponent commits a thrust, rip with a *reves*, retreating. If he returns with the same thrust, rip with a *tajo*. Whenever you come to join crossed with the opponent with nails-up or nails-down, flourish with *tajos* and *reveses* from the wrist to the head very often, the quillons never leaving from the front of the face, nor giving color to the arm, moving only the wrist. In the last one, go backwards with a *tajo* to the shins.

Chapter One-Hundred Thirty-Eight

If being established nails-up or in whichever manner that he would be, commit a *reves* to the head. The opponent, before the *reves* passes, gives a nails-up thrust in the eyes, as was well-declared before. When said thrust is committed, if he that raised with the *reves* lowers to defend it, free below and give a *reves* in the head with the wrist. Take note of this *reves*.

Chapter One-Hundred Thirty-Nine

Whenever the two are crossed above, whichever of them is able to leave with a *reves* to the legs, the opponent can guard the leg and give a nails-up thrust in the eyes. He who gives the *reves* does not have to be sudden, but falling from the posture where it is, without more movement in the air – Note that every time you will be uncovered, the opponent can give a nails-up thrust in the chest – If you already go to defend pressing, take care that he doesn't leave against you with a *reves* before you arrive.

Chapter One-Hundred Forty: On the Many Ways the *Reves* to the Head and Legs Is Defended

f.59

That the reveses are given in many manners

Since in some posture before, nails-up or nails-down, mention is made of leaving from it with a *reves*, no more or less than a *tajo*, he who understands the weapons understands that since the *reves* left from the posture established nails-up, it seems false; to *diestros*, there are no false techniques[97] in terms of attacking, because if they are *diestros*, they must understand the lack that exists.

The reves received nails-up in order to leave with another equal, but it has no place going to the head

Understanding it, one can easily attend to the remedy, wanting to offend the opponent as much, and more that the *reveses* cannot leave otherwise from said posture, and not from the pocket. When they leave from this posture, each one has an obligation to know the false and the good of the play: The false, not in order to use it, but to be guarded from it, and the good in order to take advantage of it. Then, armed nails-up, if the opponent commits a low *reves* to the leg, guard the foot so that the blow passes and give a nails-up thrust in the eyes.

Chapter One-Hundred Forty-One

The same *reves* that we said before can be given when, being established nails-up, the opponent tests, to which is given the same counter in the eyes, which you do not make with movement of the sword, but only shaking. One can defend the same *reves* by giving a nails-up thrust before the opponent's sword passes to the outside. While moving the hand in order to give it, the same thrust is given nails-up below the arm in the armpit before the sword passes, which makes two wounds: The thrust and the opponent dropping the sword arm making a wound – but if the *reves* passes to the outside, it can be defended by going to the head with a nails-down thrust to the eyes. As for me, I would put in the left foot, loading the body to the left side. When the *reves* passes, a *reves* can be given in the elbow with the wrist, retreating.

The counters are not written here, because they are already given in another place.

f.60

Chapter One-Hundred Forty-Two

In another way, if they only take the crossing parry, turn then with a nails-up thrust above the sword – if this *reves* descends to the legs, run with a nails-down thrust to the thigh or to the belly. If instead you only want to parry crossing low, as soon as you cross, turn to thrust nails-up to the thigh below the sword.

If the opponent raises with a *tajo*, raise a nails-up thrust to the eyes. If he raises with a *reves* to the head, raise nails-down to the eyes (at least raise to the parry). When you cross low, if you don't want to give said nails-up thrust below the sword, raise a nails-down thrust to the eyes, giving a sudden jump well to your left side and reaching to the opponent – or reaching to the opponent, give a *reves* in the head, or retreating backwards, give a *reves* in the sword arm, or entering, give a *tajo* in the face with the wrist, or retreating a little, give a nails-up thrust in the waist with the wrist, or as soon as this *reves* arrives, one can give a *reves* with *mandoble* in the head.

Chapter One-Hundred Forty-Three

When the *reves* passes, one can guard the foot very well and give a *tajo* in the head with the wrist – giving a *reves* in the head in the same manner. When they lift the foot for these blows, it does not have to be more than enough that the opponent's *reves* passes, and then at the same time return to set it down with said blow. He who remains below the opponent's sword with his can free by the point and give a *tajo* in the face. When the opponent throws a *tajo* to the legs, go to the low crossing parry, then leave by the point with a *reves* to the face, entering suddenly.

How One Will Know Whether the *Reves* Goes High or Low

Note that when the *reves* goes to the head, he that plays it leans with the body in order to reach, and puts himself in somewhat, but that which goes to the leg is not put in, by not staying below the opponent's sword. By that, the knowledge of the *reves* which goes to the head, and that which goes to the leg, is clear.

Chapter One-Hundred Forty-Four: Doubled Lessons f.62[98]

The two established in whatever posture that may be, either nails-up or nails-down, if the opponent rips your sword, free as much as you can and commit a nails-up thrust to the eyes. If the opponent presses on the thrust, give a *reves*, retreating backwards. If the opponent continues the nails-up thrust to the chest, rip it with a *tajo* to the head. If the opponent retreats, and the *tajo* passes in vain, and he returns with the same nails-up thrust, defend it with a nails-down thrust to the chest, putting in the right or left foot. If the opponent turns his foot back to thrust nails-up, continue to thrust nails-up to the chest by the same edges. If he turns to press on said sword on your right side, give him a nails-down thrust in the belly in the manner of *balanzada*.

Chapter One-Hundred Forty-Five

Established nails-down or nails-up, if the opponent tests, leave with a *reves* to the legs, retreating. If the opponent defends it with a nails-up thrust to the chest, defend with a nails-up thrust by the same edges. If the opponent presses on the sword, respond with a threatening *reves* to the head. If the opponent parries, leave with a ripped *tajo*. If the opponent retreats, and the sword passes in vain, and he commits a nails-up thrust to the chest or to the face, give a *balanzada.*

Chapter One-Hundred Forty-Six: *Tajos* Are Given in Many Manners

The two established, throw a long *tajo*, withdrawing the foot with the blow. If the opponent throws another and withdraws, give a nails-down or nails-up thrust to the chest. If the opponent rips it with a *tajo*, parry crossing and then leave with a *tajo*, retreating. If the opponent continues to thrust nails-up, rip with a *tajo*. If he returns with said nails-up thrust, rip with a *reves*.

Chapter One-Hundred Forty-Seven

Before you establish, if the opponent throws a *tajo,* throw a *reves* after this *tajo*. If the opponent returns with a *reves*, return with a *tajo* from
f.63 low to high, in a manner that it cuts from the knee to the head, and after this another ordinary tajo while retreating.

If the opponent continues with a nails-up thrust when the *tajo* passes, rip it with a *tajo*. If the opponent retreats, returning with the same nails-up thrust, defend it by the same edges. If the opponent turns the hand nails-down, press on the sword. If the opponent leaves with a *reves*, leave with a *reves* to the elbow. This *reves* will be defended by turning from the wrist with a thrust to the eyes. If the opponent gives a *balanzada*, turn the foot back and give a *tajo* in the face. If the opponent raised for the parry, turn and give a nails-down thrust in the belly. If the opponent leaves the foot back to thrust nails-up to the eyes, press to your right side. If the opponent leaves by the point with a *reves*, before he leaves, give a nails-down thrust in the face.

Locked Fight

Those that understand this, take note that in a lasting fight, it is not enough to commit a blow alone, but one has an obligation to respond to the opponent's blows and arm a play in which he may come to fall.

Chapter One-Hundred Forty-Eight: Rules for Lefties[99]

Being a lefty armed in the nails-up posture, if one commits a nails-up thrust to the chest, defend it with a nails-down thrust to the same chest. This thrust can be defended by retreating a little back and giving a nails-up thrust in the chest, freed below, which the opponent can defend with a nails-up thrust by the same edges.

Take note that whenever one is armed nails-down, he has to be offended by the opponent inside nails-up, and being armed nails-up, he has to be offended outside, nails-up to the chest. Note

Chapter One-Hundred Forty-Nine

Being established like this, if one lowers the sword to the outside, the opponent can give a nails-down thrust. If he places the sword to the inside, commit a nails-up thrust to the chest, which can be defended by ripping with a *tajo*. This *tajo* can be defended with a nails-down thrust to the chest, and if ripping with a *reves*, with a nails-up thrust to the chest. Being established nails-up, one of them can also test the f.64
opponent's sword. If he leaves with a *reves* to the legs, it is defended by guarding the foot and leg where the *reves* goes and giving a nails-up thrust in the face, or *tajo* in the head, or *reves* in the same place. One can also give a nails-up thrust in the thigh if the *reves* goes to the leg.

Chapter One-Hundred Fifty

Established nails-up, one of them lowers the sword. If the opponent comes with a nails-up thrust to the eyes, commit the same nails-down thrust inside to the chest. If he is established nails-down, one of them commits a nails-up thrust below his sword to the eyes. If the opponent defends it nails-up, turn quickly to where it started and give the same nails-up thrust outside. Established nails-up, if one of them presses on the opponent's sword to the outside, commit a *reves* to the head, and if the opponent parries, turn with a *tajo* to the same place, the quillons remaining high.

Chapter One-Hundred Fifty-One

Established nails-up, if the opponent presses your sword on the inside, leave with a *tajo* to the head. If the opponent parries, leave with a *reves* to the head, quillons high — being established nails-up, a *tajo* can also be thrown to the legs. If the opponent parries low, turn with a nails-down thrust to the thigh, freed with the wrist below his sword. If the opponent withdraws the leg and leaves with a *tajo* to the head, raise a nails-down thrust to the eyes. If the opponent didn't raise, and you don't want to give the thrust in the thigh, leave with a *reves*. The opponent will parry this *reves*; as soon as he takes the parry, turn the sword and give a nails-up thrust in the chest.

Chapter One-Hundred Fifty-Two

Established nails-up, if the opponent throws a *reves* to the legs, guard the leg and give a *tajo*, *reves*, or a nails-up thrust in the head.

f.65 Established nails-up, if the opponent throws a ripped *tajo*, retreat in step so that it passes in vain and give a nails-up thrust in the face.

Established nails-up or nails-down in whatever manner that the opponent throws a *tajo*, when the *tajo* raised, commit a nails-down thrust to the eyes. In the same manner, if the opponent lifts with a *reves*, at the point of lifting, give a nails-up thrust in the face.

Chapter One-Hundred Fifty-Three

Being established nails-up, if the opponent gains your sword, free by the point and give a *tajo* in the face, entering suddenly (this *tajo* is given when he gains from inside to outside). If the opponent commits a *tajo* to your face that you leave uncovered, turn nails-down with a thrust to the eyes. The same if the opponent gains it to your inside, leave by the point and *reves* to the face. If he attacks you with a *tajo*, turn nails-up. If the opponent throws a *reves* to the legs, turn taking the parry low, thrust nails-up to the chest, or *reves* to the arm, leaving – you can give a *reves* in the face or a *tajo* in the same place with the wrist.

Note that all these four techniques have to leave by the point of the opponent's sword, and these last two, the more you enter, the better and safer it is.

Chapter One-Hundred Fifty-Four

Established nails-up, give a blow below the quillons, in the wrist, retreating. When the opponent gives a nails-up thrust, press on the sword to one side. If he frees, when he's leaving, give a nails-up thrust in the face, not entering, but being thrown with only the arm.

Established nails-up, one of them passes the sword to the opponent's right side, or plays a lost *tajo*, and if the opponent commits a nails-up thrust, free the sword below to the side where he was before and give a nails-up thrust by the same edges. If the opponent presses on the sword, leave with a *reves* or *tajo*, whichever will suit the posture.

Established nails-up, if the opponent throws a *tajo*, when he raises, give a blow in the crook of the elbow or thrust nails-down in the face. You can do the same if he throws a *reves*, giving a blow in the arm, retreating, or a nails-up thrust in the eyes with the quillons high. f.66

Chapter One-Hundred Fifty-Five

Established in whichever posture, throw a *tajo* to the legs. If the opponent parries, quickly turn nails-down above his sword and give a nails-down thrust in the chest. If the opponent raises with a *tajo* to the head, raise and give the same thrust in the face. If one wants, he can quit the thrust and leave, cutting a *tajo* to the thigh.[100] Whenever they are established nails-up and one of them lowers, the opponent can give a blow in the crook of the elbow, retreating. Established in whichever posture that they will throw a *tajo* to the legs, the opponent can defend it with a nails-down thrust to the thigh.

Chapter One-Hundred Fifty-Six

Established nails-up, one of them lowers the sword. If the opponent attacks with a nails-up thrust, give a *balanzada*. The counters to the *balanzadas* are on folio 53, Chapter One-hundred Twenty-two. One can do the same whenever the opponent commits a high nails-up thrust.

Established nails-up or nails-down, if the opponent presses your sword to the outside, turn with the wrist by the point of the opponent's sword and give a nails-down thrust in the chest. The opponent can press this thrust over his left arm, and give that which was right before, and give a *reves* in the face. The enemy pressing, if the opponent turns with a *tajo* to the head, parry with a nails-down thrust to the eyes.

Note that when the opponent is armed nails-up, don't allow him to be on the outside.

In What Posture They Have to Have the Sword

When he is nails-down, don't allow him to be on the inside, because when the opponent is nails-down, you are nails-up on the inside, and when nails-up, you are nails-down outside, and you will be safe.

PART TWO: SWORD AND SHIELD

First Chapter on the Shield: Advice for the Shieldman

f.67

First, the shieldman has to take note that when coming against a dagger, all his play has to be outside –

How the double arms are distinct, and the play isn't

He also takes note that whenever he plays with two or more, that all the thrusts thrown against the opponents on the right side are nails-down, and he will be defended by the same (with nails-down) from their blows, not taking any of their blows on the shield. Take note that one does much so that they will not be at the sides, but in front, or to one side.

That the same techniques[101] of the single sword are parries

Chapter Two

Take note that in battling against two swords, one has to keep to the rule of shield against dagger, ordinarily deflecting the opponent's sword with the shield. Take note that, if one is attacked by many in a plaza or a wide field, that he doesn't establish, but rips from one side to the other, as the manner that will be seen in this part will be dealt with in its place. Take note that if one is attacked by a *montante*, that it is possible to battle safely, but being able to withdraw is best; when one does not, take the parry on the shield and attack below with a thrust. Take note that if one is attacked by a single sword, that he does not have to keep to the rule of the shield, but to present the chest[102] to the attacker, undoing his blows and attacking to one side and the other.

Chapter Three

For one that gives battle with double arms,[103] it is very necessary not to drop the cloak (if it will be possible, out of his hand), but to ready it at the same time with the shield, buckler, and dagger; neither should the scabbard remain in the street, nor the hat, because by these signs they won't come to know of the cause having something (meaning at night). As such, the *montante* will not be taken from home with a cloak, but with the light scabbard, testing it first.

Chapter Four

f.68

Established nails-down, the shield will be in front of the chest, one palm[104] distant, with the arm circled, and the right breast uncovered. If the opponent tests the sword, before it arrives, give a *reves* in the leg, not taking the shield from its place. The enemy can lift the leg, so that it passes in vain, and thrust nails-up to the chest, which the opponent can defend by the same edges with a nails-up thrust. The opponent can undo this thrust to his right side with the shield and give a nails-down thrust in the thigh, putting in the left foot, covering with the left face of the shield.

Chapter Five

The two established nails-up, if the opponent commits a nails-up thrust to the chest, take the sword on your shield, raising it at the same time to the head, lifting the arm well, and give a nails-up thrust in the belly, not entering more than enough that the thrust reaches. The opponent can defend this thrust by undoing it with the shield to the left side and give a nails-down thrust in the belly, putting in the foot and placing the shield to the left face.

Chapter Six

Whenever the two swords cross, you can to give a nails-down thrust in the belly, giving the shield to the opponent's sword, putting yourself below yours so that the head remains covered. In response to this thrust, the opponent can retreat the foot back, offering a nails-up thrust to the eyes, which you can deflect with a *tajo* with the sword, or at the time that the opponent retreats (with deflection), leave the deflection and give a *tajo* in the face, because he remains uncovered from that side.

Chapter Seven

Established whichever way, one of them throws a long *tajo* below the shield, withdrawing the foot. If the opponent throws another, respond to it with a *reves*. If the opponent throws another *reves*, respond with another *reves,* and another, and another, placing the shield to that side where the opponent's *reveses* can offend when they come, which is
f.69 to the right side of the face, the *reveses* occurring in time so that they don't meet each other, and when the opponent's passes, put yourself below the shield, with the shield in its place, and give the same *reves* that you went playing outside, but in the legs, putting yourself in, or

at the time that the opponent's *reves* passes, turn from the wrist with a *tajo* to the head. Note that when you give this *tajo*, it has to be when your sword goes over the head in order to begin to descend, while said *tajo* turns, because then the opponent's sword is starting to come up.

Chapter Eight

Keeping to this same rule from Chapter Seven, you can, in place of a *tajo*, give a nails-up thrust in the chest with the wrist, turning the sword how you turn it for the *tajo*. Note that if the two throw their *reveses* in the form that when one goes with his sword over the head in order to descend, the other goes with the sword rounding close to the floor in order to raise, this is where the thrust, *tajo*, and *reves* of which we speak can be committed safely and without danger.

Chapter Nine

Being established nails-up or nails-down, if the opponent tests your sword, rip with the shield and commit a ripped *reves* to the head. You will do the same if he goes with a nails-up thrust to the eyes after testing. The opponent can parry the *reves* with the shield and give a nails-down thrust in the belly, entering with the left foot. When the opponent comes with a nails-up thrust as said above, you can undo it with the shield to the right side and give a nails-down thrust in the thigh, putting in the left foot.

Chapter Ten

Established nails-up, if the opponent rips a *tajo* to the legs, take the sword and join it like this: The shield hand and the guard hand together, fingernails to fingernails, so that the shield remains over the sword, and pressing it to where the *tajo* comes, you will take the parry in this manner. If the opponent turns with a *reves* to the legs, give a nails-down thrust in the thigh. If he doesn't turn with a *reves*, but raises with a *tajo* to the head, raise the shield to the blow, take the parry, and give a nails-down thrust at the same time in the thigh or belly as quickly as possible.

Chapter Eleven f.70

Being established nails-up or nails-down, the opponent tests the sword.

Before it arrives, give a nails-down thrust in the thigh, remaining uncovered by the shield on the right side. If the opponent commits a *reves* to the head, or a thrust, give him another nails-down thrust, but parrying with the shield that previously had stayed and left you uncovered. You can, when they go to test, not give said thrust, but give him a *tajo* in the knee,[105] entering suddenly to the side of the same right knee, remaining uncovered. If he comes with a *reves* to the head, you will make use of the counter above.

Chapter Twelve

Established nails-down or nails-up, if the opponent goes to test, deflect with the shield and give a *reves* to the head. The opponent can parry this *reves* in the shield and at the same time give him a *reves* in the sword arm, retreating back. From firm to firm, when the opponent runs the *reves*, he can also take it crossed, and then put himself in below the shield and give a nails-down thrust in the belly or a *reves* in the legs.

Chapter Thirteen

If established, or in whatever manner that the opponent rips a *tajo* to your head, take the parry, lifting the shield above your head, and give a nails-up thrust in the chest. If they don't offer said nails-up thrust, but only take the parry on the shield, the opponent will then turn with a *reves* to the head. When the opponent comes with the *tajo*, you can put yourself below the shield and give a nails-down thrust in the belly or in the thigh.

Chapter Fourteen

Established, if the opponent rips a *tajo* and it goes to the head, you can take only the parry in the shield, uncovering the chest, and remain armed nails-down. If the opponent turns to thrust nails-up to the chest below the shield, undo it with the shield to the right side and, entering a little bit, give a nails-down thrust in the belly. Established in whatever posture that one may be, if you commit a nails-up thrust
f.71 and the opponent goes to rip it with a *tajo*, free the sword and run with the same thrust as from before.

Note that you will keep to this rule all the times that you will commit a thrust and the opponent rips it with the sword, freeing without the swords meeting, if possible.

Chapter Fifteen

Established nails-up or nails-down, commit a nails-up thrust to the eyes. If the opponent undoes it with the shield, free quickly and give a nails-down thrust in the belly, putting in the left foot (if you give it nails-up, it is not necessary to put in the foot).

In place of the low thrust, you can give a nails-up thrust in the face, which is the same that you would have committed, and this is not bad. You can give this same nails-up thrust below the arm, or in the belly, rounding the sword above the shield when he goes to deflect.

Whenever the opponent throws a *tajo* or rips a *tajo*, you will be able to wait for the *tajo* with your sword in the way to parry, then give a *reves* in the face from that place. Before this blow is given, the opponent will be able to give a nails-down thrust in the belly, putting himself in, leaving the shield on the head.

Chapter Sixteen

Established in whatever posture that one may be, if the opponent commits a nails-up thrust, rip with a *tajo*. If the opponent frees and runs with the same thrust, deflect with the shield with a *reves*. When you go to rip with a *tajo*, if the opponent frees the thrust and goes ahead with it, undo it with the shield without a *reves*, but the same *tajo* goes running its course to the legs without stopping, in a manner that the deflection doesn't impede the *tajo*. Note this blow well and slowly.

Chapter Seventeen

Established nails-up, gain the opponent's sword below and give a *reves* in the legs, putting yourself in below the shield. The opponent can take this *reves* crossing low. When the *reves* will be defended, turn with the wrist to thrust nails-up to the belly above his sword and retreat somewhat when you free. The opponent can deflect this thrust with the sword, retreating.

f.70

Chapter Eighteen: Declares in what Form the Counters Go

Those that read the counters of these rules of the shield must take note that they are mixed in the same chapters and are the responses in the same chapters when the opponent attacks and the second defends, in such a manner that the blow and counter of it are all mixed in each chapter.

Chapter Nineteen

Established nails-up, if the opponent throws a nails-up thrust to the eyes, rip with a *tajo* to the head. If the opponent parries by lifting the shield, as soon as he begins to lift, quit the *tajo* and give a nails-up thrust below the arm. When you refute with a *tajo*, if the opponent comes with said nails-up thrust, you can also turn to deflect with the shield with a *reves* to the legs.

Chapter Twenty

Established nails-up, threaten the same thrust to the eyes. If the opponent deflects with the shield, or even if he does not deflect it, if he takes it on the shield covering his sight, give the same nails-down thrust in the belly, covering yourself with the shield. Established as we said nails-up, if the opponent deflects the posture with a *tajo*, or if he commits it from firm to firm, retreat so that his *tajo* passes in vain, and in passing, run a spirited nails-up thrust to the eyes or chest. This thrust is defended by ripping with a *tajo* or *reves* with the shield, or better, undoing it with the shield to the right side and giving a nails-down thrust in the thigh, putting in the left foot quickly.

Chapter Twenty-One

Established nails-up, if the opponent attacks with a *reves*, give him a *reves* in the elbow when it passes, while retreating. If the opponent continues with a nails-up thrust to the chest, rip it with a *tajo* with the sword.

When you go with a ripped *tajo*, if the opponent parries on the shield and gives a nails-down thrust in the belly while putting in a foot, round your sword above his sword and give him a nails-up thrust below the left arm, taking the right foot back. Being established, if he throws a *tajo*, give him a *tajo* in the sword arm in the crook of the elbow at the time that he lifts, retreating, or thrust nails-up in the chest, giving the shield to the parry, leaving with ripped *tajo* and *reves*. f.73

Chapter Twenty-Two

Established nails-up, if the opponent deflects with a *tajo* to the shins, take the parry on the sword, joining it nails-up with the shield hand, with the shield thrown above the shield, and the point of the sword inclined toward the floor. The sword touching yours, give a *reves* in the opponent's right leg, then withdraw the sword to the place from which you took it. If the opponent lifts with a *tajo* before you went with the *reves*, attack with a nails-down thrust in the belly and cover well with the shield above the head.

Chapter Twenty-Three

Established nails-down, if the opponent tests the sword, play a *reves* to the legs before it arrives. If the opponent guards the leg and continues the same thrust, deflect it with the shield and go with the same *reves* to the legs. If the opponent returns to guard the leg and continues the same nails-up thrust to the eyes, rip with a *tajo* to the legs with the sword, or follow his thrust with a nails-up thrust by the same edges. The opponent can undo this with the shield and give a nails-down thrust in the thigh, putting in the foot and covering the head with the shield.

Chapter Twenty-Four

Putting the shield in front of the chest and the sword below it, over the left leg with the point to the floor, the quillons covered below it, if the opponent commits a nails-up thrust to the eyes, lift the shield, taking the thrust on it, pressing it well to the left side, and give a nails-up thrust in the chest without putting in a foot, or rip it with a *reves*.

Note that although it is mentioned that you give the thrusts in the chest, those in the belly or lower are much better, because those that go to the chest will be easy for the opponent to undo with the shield. So in my advice, all the nails-up thrusts that have to go to the chest will be better lower, having a place. Note

f.74

Chapter Twenty-Five

Established in whatever manner that one may be, if the opponent comes with a *reves* to the head, turn the shield back, putting in the left foot, and give a nails-down thrust in the chest or eyes. Note that the thrust is enough for the parry, and take note that the head stays behind the quillons, not in front, when you give the nails-down thrust. When you give the thrust, bend at the knees, not with the body. You can do the same when the opponent commits a nails-up thrust to the eyes; deflect it with the shield to the right side and at the same time give a *tajo* in the knees, retreating.

Chapter Twenty-Six

When established nails-down, if the opponent tests your sword, run a *tajo* to the knees or thigh before it arrives. If the opponent turns with a *reves* to the head withdrawing the leg, take the blow on the shield and give a nails-down thrust in the same place, putting yourself in somewhat, and leave cutting.

Chapter Twenty-Seven

Whenever the opponent tests your sword, free below and give him a nails-up thrust in the sword shoulder. If the opponent deflects it with the shield, give the counter that is given in this place. When they test, one can free by the point of the sword and give a *tajo* in the face. Note that the opponent can take the blow on the shield and offend below.

Chapter Twenty-Eight

Established in whatever manner that one may be, if the opponent tests your sword, go before it arrives and press on his in the manner that you arm a *reves*. If he leaves with it, give one of the counters that are given to the *reveses*. Established nails-up, if the opponent commits a nails-up thrust, defend it by the same edges. If the opponent presses this second thrust with his sword to the right side, leave with a *reves* to the leg. If the opponent continues to thrust nails-up, turn to him with the same nails-up thrust by the edges or rip it with a *tajo*.

Chapter Twenty-Nine

f.75

Established in whatever manner that one may be when the opponent throws a *tajo* to the legs, if you parry with the sword below the shield and the point to the floor, take note that the opponent that played the *tajo*[106] can turn with the wrist with a nails-down thrust to the right thigh, placing this thrust with the wrist. When it starts to leave with the sword circling the hand, one can go with the sword close to the face, circling with much speed. When they circle the sword, if the opponent doesn't lift the shield in order to cover from the sword that circles, stop going to the thigh and give the thrust in the face, and then leave with *tajo* and *reves*.

Chapter Thirty: How to Move the Shield and Its Parries

It is no less necessary to declare in what posture the shield has to be moved, as there are different parries for different blows:

Note that when you arm yourself nails-up with the sword in front of the chest, you have to have the shield in front of the left breast, one palm[107] away from the body; it will go in the same place when one is armed nails-down with the sword in front of the chest.

When one arms nails-up low, with the point of the sword to the floor, the shield will be above the hand and quillons, in front of the belly, half a palm distant. When you establish nails-up with the sword in front of the belly, put the shield almost over the head to the left side.

The Parries:
When the opponent throws a *reves* to the head, pass the whole shield to the right side so that it covers all of the face, and you see the enemy on the left side;

Against the *tajo*, the shield is in front of the left side of the face, so that you see the opponent on the right side;

For the *tajo* to the legs, the shield goes above the quillons of the sword, next to the belly, and with a *reves* the same, in a manner that the parries don't have to be taken on the edge of the shield as many have said, but in the body of it, nor do they have to put it in front of the eyes, nor is the shield obligated to take any blow from the waist down;

only the dagger can do it, while the buckler takes them on its rim.

f.76 ## Chapter Thirty-One

Deflecting with a *reves* to the legs, if the opponent takes the parry below the shield with the point of the sword on the floor as said before, let the *reves* be in the head or in the sword arm. You can do the same if you go with a *tajo* – the opponent going to take the parry as said above, let the *tajo* be in the head. If the opponent does not take the parry as it is said, but withdraws the leg and comes with a nails-up thrust above, rip with a *tajo*. When you threw the *tajo* to the legs, if the opponent returns with a *reves*, at the passing of the sword, give a nails-up thrust as well as the sword is below the shield. If the opponent leaves stepping backwards, continue with a nails-up thrust to the belly with the shield high, which takes the free blow.

Chapter Thirty-Two

Whenever the opponent throws a fast *tajo*, put yourself in below the shield and give a nails-down thrust in the belly on arriving, or at the time that it rises, give a nails-up thrust in the chest, taking the blow on the shield. You can do the same if the opponent comes with a *reves*, putting yourself in with a nails-down thrust to the belly or lower, giving the shield to the blow on the right side. Established nails-up or nails-down, deflect with a *reves* to the legs. If the opponent withdraws the leg and continues to thrust nails-up to the chest, turn and deflect with a *reves* to the head. Note that these two deflections with a *reves* are with the shield and not with the sword.

Chapter Thirty-Three

Established nails-up or committing a thrust, if the opponent deflects with a *tajo* to the head, take the blow on the shield in the air with the sword below it, the point remaining to the opponent, and taking the blow, let the sword fall with a *reves* to the legs. You can do the same with a deflecting *reves*, taking the blow in the same manner, and in taking it, to let the sword fall with a *tajo* to the legs, not forgetting where the shield has to remain. When the *reves* is given to the legs, the opponent can give a nails-down thrust in the thigh with the sword below the shield.

f.77 One can do the same when the opponent lets the *tajo* fall to the legs, taking the blow on the sword below the shield and giving a thrust in the thigh.

Chapter Thirty-Four

The two established nails-up, the opponent gains the sword above, making the *garatusa*, circling above his sword and entering at the same time with a nails-down thrust in the thigh, or having only gained the sword, the opponent frees with the same thrust as it is said, and puts the shield to the opponent's right side. Established nails-up, if he comes with a *reves*, the opponent can take the parry on the sword from nails-up, running his by the edges and arriving to the opponent and giving a ripped *reves* along his side in the thigh, putting the shield on the head.

Chapter Thirty-Five

Established nails-up, if the opponent tests the sword, the opponent can give a *tajo* in the elbow or thigh. He can do the same, being established nails-down with the shield open from the chest; if the opponent commits a nails-up thrust to the chest, you can deflect it with the shield to the right side and at the same time give a *tajo* in the shins, entering somewhat with the blow, in a manner that the deflection and the *tajo* and the step all have to be at one point.

Note this blow well, which is no more than an exchange of arms: The right to the left side, and the left to the right side.

Chapter Thirty-Six

The two established, one of them will put his sword over his left leg, nails-down, and the shield over his right arm, turned sideways to the left with the shoulder uncovered to the opponent. If the opponent commits a *reves* or thrust to said shoulder, one can turn, directing the shield to the blow, with a *reves* in the legs, entering a little suddenly.

Being established, if one of them throws a *tajo* which will pass in vain, and the opponent comes with a thrust or *reves* to the shoulder, give the above counter. If you throw a *reves* which passes in vain, and the opponent comes with a nails-up thrust, rip it with a *tajo*. f.78

f.79

Chapter Thirty-Seven

Established nails-up, test the opponent's sword on the second third. If the opponent consents, leave by the point of his sword with a *reves* to the legs. When it leaves (before it leaves), the opponent will give a nails-down thrust in the thigh –

but after it left, ignore this comment

One can stop leaving with said *reves* and give a nails-up thrust in the thigh, staying with a parry to the left side with one's shield. This thrust and *reves* have to be entering somewhat, and against the thrust that is given in the thigh, one has the same thrust in the thigh as a counter.

Chapter Thirty-Eight

Whenever the two come together, crossed high, nails-down, one of them may give a nails-up thrust in the face, turning the hand at the wrist above the opponent's sword. If the opponent turns with a nails-up thrust to the face, rip it to your right side with the shield, freeing the sword that goes dealing with the opponent's, and give a nails-down thrust in the thigh or belly, putting the shield in its place. Note that the low thrusts are given such that the hand always remains below the shield.

Chapter Thirty-Nine

Two shieldmen established, one of them may put the shield with the edge on the waist, drop the edge that is toward the air toward the floor, and put his sword nails-down with the arm a little open. If the opponent comes with a nails-up thrust to the eyes, lift the shield, gaining said thrust on it, lifting it above the head, and give a nails-up thrust in the thigh or belly. If the opponent attacks the left side that goes uncovered, attend to it with the sword to that side with the point to the floor and the shield above the quillons, as already dealt with, keeping the hands together with the parts inside.

Chapter Forty

Established nails-up or down, when you gain the opponent's sword, if he leaves with a *reves* to the head, take the blow on the edge of the shield and give him a *reves* in the legs. This same technique can be given when the opponent rips with a *reves*. If ripping with a *tajo*, give the same *tajo* in the legs, being quick in the parry.

How the Sword Hand has to be When One will give a Nails-Down Thrust in the Thigh or Belly

Note that when presenting the nails-down thrust (which is dealt with many times before) to be given in the belly or thigh, the quillons hand always has to remain either behind the shield or below the inside, because remaining outside is dangerous.

Chapter Forty-One

Whenever the opponent goes to rip a nails-up thrust, before he arrives with his sword to yours, set off with the same *tajo* to the waist, taking the *tajo* on your shield. You can also give this *tajo* in the head, and *reves* in the sword arm.

Chapter Forty-Two

Established nails-up, if the opponent is armed in a high posture with nails-up, arm yourself in the same nails-up posture, but much lower than his. If he commits a nails-up thrust to the eyes, beat it with the shield and, without entering, give a nails-up thrust in the thigh, retreating after. If the opponent continues to thrust nails-up, rip with a *tajo*, rip with a *reves* to the legs, or give a nails-down thrust to the belly.

Chapter Forty-Three

Keeping to the order of Chapter Seven, when the sword goes close to the floor in order to rise, stop raising and from there commit a *tajo* to the opponent's legs or sword arm. With this *tajo*, the farther back your sword goes, the better it leaves, and the more secure the *tajo*.

How from Each of These Rules, Masters Can Deliver Diverse Lessons, Because All Are Doubled

The *diestro* or the master takes note that since there are a certain amount of these rules of the shield, one can have different lessons and techniques from each of them, if at each blow they will leave with their counters.

Chapter Forty-Four

He that professes the use of these arms has to have much care and advice in intending to be armed in all occasions before the opponent. Armed when the opponent begins arming himself, attack him with
f.80
much vigor with a nails-down or nails-up thrust, a *tajo,* or *reves* (whichever is better at the time), lifting the shield to the uncovered part and retreating with the same advice to be placed in his posture.

Chapter Forty-Five: How with the Thrust, *Tajo*, and *Reves*, They Can Defend Against Whichever of the Opponent's Blows, and with Each One Itself

Established in whatever posture that one will be, if the opponent attacks you with a nails-up or nails-down thrust to the chest, you can undo it to the right side and give another nails-down thrust in the belly, undoing his with the shield to the right side like I say. If you don't want to respond with a thrust, respond with a *reves* to the legs. If you don't want to respond with a *reves*, respond with a *tajo*. Note that these *tajos* and *reveses* don't have to be rounding above the head, but sneaking below. You can do the same if he attacks you with a *tajo*, giving either a thrust, *tajo,* or *reves*. You can do the same if he attacks you with a *reves*, giving a *reves, tajo,* or thrust, keeping to the rule above. Take note that this *tajo*, thrust, and *reves* have to be from the waist down.

all the techniques[108] in double arms are better low

Chapter Forty-Six:[109] Two Blows In One Time

Being established nails-up, if the opponent throws a *reves*, you can give a nails-down thrust in the belly in counter without moving the arm, descending with a *reves* to the sword arm in a manner that, when the opponent starts off with the *reves*, you will descend to said thrust, cutting a *reves* in the arm without making two movements. In place of the thrust, you can give a *reves* in the thigh, and thus give two *reveses*, one in the arm, another in the thigh. The counters already go in their place.

Chapter Forty-Seven

Established nails-up, if the opponent tests, free by the outside of the point with the wrist, entering with a step of the right foot, and give a nails-down thrust in the thigh, keeping the shield parrying the left side. This thrust is defended by taking back the right foot and giving a nails-up thrust rounded on the right side.

PART THREE: SWORD AND BUCKLER

Declaration on the Buckler, First Chapter: How the Small Buckler is not a Safe Arm f.81

I remember hearing it said that the only arms were sword alone, and sword and shield, and there are not many times that there was notice of sword and dagger, or sword and buckler. There is no lack of those curious that, moved by lawful or unlawful opportunities, will invent buckler and dagger, taking from the shield the play which is shown now. For the benefit of the masters, and somewhat of the senior master,[110] they make one weapon three, being really one regarding the blows, inasmuch as the three are distinct: Shield, dagger, and buckler. Because of that, those who have lost interest understand that whoever plays well with the shield (as it is queen)[111] will be excused from learning dagger or buckler, as he can use the same play in whichever of said weapons, save that one differentiates the placement of the buckler and taking of the parries.

Second Chapter: How the Parries will be Taken and the Buckler Held

He that will give battle with sword and buckler is obliged to hold the buckler arm long and straight, because if he holds it withdrawn, the elbow remains uncovered, and going straight, it cannot be injured. When taking the parries, he doesn't wait for the opponent's sword to come to it; he is obliged to halt the blow in its path. Stated more clearly, the buckler-man is obliged to seek the opponent's sword when it comes with the blow, because as it is so small, one can be swiftly deceived in the parry and, taking care that it is parried, become injured, so said diligence has to be made.

Third Chapter: How One Commits the Thrusts from the Belt Down f.82

Whenever it happens that one has occasion to commit a thrust to the lower parts, when in the shield we say that such thrusts have to be given nails-down, due to the shield being very wide, it always goes covering the sword hand, even though it goes nails-down. With such thrusts committed with buckler, it is necessary that they go nails-up so the quillons hand is protected.

Fourth Chapter: That One Can Excuse Putting In the Left Foot

We deal with many rules in the shield that necessarily had to have the left foot put in; with a buckler, it is enough that when the left foot has to enter, the right enters, because as it is small, the pass from one side to the other does not impede the sight when it goes in front of the face or takes the parries on the edge.

Chapter Five

With the buckler, one can put to use Rule Forty-Five of the shield, on folio Eighty. Taking in all the step and form of attack and in defending the *tajo*, as well as the *reves*, as well as the thrust, keeping in all to the rule of the buckler in the manner that it has to move, as dealt with before.

Chapter Six[112]

PART FOUR: TWO SWORDS

First Chapter on the Two Swords in Rules: A Street that is not Very Narrow, in the Front f.83

Drawing the two swords, the one in the left hand is withdrawn below the right arm, and the one in the right hand will be placed nails-down above the head. Putting in the left foot,[113] throw a *reves* with the left arm and a *tajo* with the right arm at the same time — these two blows ends with the left sword above the head nails-down, and the sword in the right hand below the one in the left. Then, put in the right foot with a *reves* of the right arm and a *tajo* with the left arm, the swords ending in the first posture, which is the left arm below the right, and the right nails-down above the head. These two steps done, return to do others like them, continuing the two blows of *tajo* and *reves* in said manner, always responding to each step of the foot with a *tajo* and *reves*, the swords always ending as it is said in the two steps, and during the battle, continue the step and blows without change.

If there is only one opponent, or at most two and no more, you can do this same rule with thrusts, putting the right foot in with a nails-down thrust with the right arm and a nails-up thrust with the left arm, the left sword ending below that of the right arm. Then return, putting the left foot in with a nails-down thrust with the left arm and a nails-up thrust with the right arm.[114] These two steps done, continue forward with the above order of *tajos* and *reveses*. You can also give these two nails-down punching thrusts,[115] as it is said in the single sword, giving a throwing thrust,[116] keeping to the order above, which is two thrusts at each step of the foot.

Second Rule: A Very Narrow Street f.84

In the first rule, in a street not very wide, we deal with three conditions of how the battle could be given: One with *tajo* and *reves*, another with nails-up and nails-down thrusts, another with two thrusts both nails-down. Those two manners of attacking with thrusts can be used when some person will be attacked in a street where a *reves* or *tajo* cannot be played because of the narrowness of the street, only that the thrusts from before can be given to one side and the other. But in a narrow street, the thrusts will be one in front of the other, and when one is committed nails-up, the thrust with the other arm also goes nails-up.

When it is thrown with a nails-down punching thrust, they both have to be nails-down.

Note this step

The step of the feet does not have to be one in front of the other, save that the opponent or opponents go retreating quickly, and this not being so, the step has to be with the right foot always in front.

Third Rule: Attacked on One Side and the Other – And Having the Opponents in Front

Positioned with the right sword above the head with the nails-down, and the one in the left hand below the right arm, put the right foot to the same side, not forward, cutting a *reves* with the left arm and at the same time a *tajo* with the right arm. As soon as the *tajo* and *reves* are made, lift the right foot that you have moved and place it two palms[117] in front of the left foot.

Finishing said *tajo* and *reves*, the swords end exchanged like this: The left nails-down over the head and the right below the left arm. Then, put the left foot to the same left side, with a *reves* with the right arm and a *tajo* with the left arm. The moment of said *tajo* and *reves* passed, lift the left foot that you had moved and place it two palms in front of the right foot. These two steps of left and right foot done with the two
f.85 blows of *tajo* and *reves*, you will start others in the manner above.

Note

For the understanding of these rules, it is enough to point out that one step is started with the right foot and the other with the left foot, because then the right foot turns another time and the left foot another.

Note

When you leave with the blows of *tajo*, you can also (and it will be better), first throw a nails-down punching thrust at the same time as the *tajo*, because the *tajo* leaves with more vigor, and also that they are two blows in one same time.

Two Shieldmen

Note that for two shieldmen, I find no rule that can help better than this, only that the blows have an obligation to be the lowest that they can, because if they go high, the opponents will put themselves in below the shields, taking the blows, and will enter with them; nor is any thrust used against shieldmen. Returning to the beginning, the two steps of left and right foot made, give battle with the said steps, as long as it lasts, taking note that if one retreats, it is enough to put one foot behind the other.

The First Rule Declares

In the first rule we deal with how one defends himself from his opponents in a not very narrow street, for which we give rules of *tajo*, *reves*, and thrusts. He who makes a *tajo* and *reves* with two swords will also be able to be defended by making only *reveses*, rotating them over the head, giving them with the arms very extended. Go playing continuously, making a circle with each other, taking the step with the right foot always in front.

Statement on these Rules Themselves

They have to note, that whenever they do the rule ahead, that if it is necessary to turn toward the rear, that they rotate in a continuous motion of two blows, *tajo* and *reves*, armed on the foot that remains back, and do the same rule that they would do. If surrounded, leave it and do the rule of being surrounded, and if retreating, leave the one and take the other.

Fourth Rule: Two or More in a Wide Street, and Shieldmen f.86

The swords positioned with the one in the left hand below the right arm, putting in the right foot, play a *tajo* to the right side to where you put in the foot, and at the same time leave with a *reves* with the left arm. The moment the *tajo* and *reves* cut, lift the right foot and put it in front of the left, and the sword that has played the *tajo* has to finish nails-down below the left arm. At the same time, *reves* with the left arm and *reves* with the right arm. These two *reveses* (standing firm) finished, throw a *tajo* with the left arm and a *reves* with the right arm on your right side, putting the left foot in front of the right at the same time. The *tajo* has to finish nails-up below the right arm, then *reves* with the left arm and *reves* with the right arm. Then start the same step as the first, then another like the second, and as many more as will be necessary, in a manner that this rule can be used with he that uses the 3rd rule.

And it can be used like the third

In summary, in this rule the foot has to be placed to the right side, and a *reves* with the left arm and *tajo* with the right arm has to be played, and this *tajo* has to cut the opponents' on the left side, at the same time lifting the right foot and putting it in front of the left. Placing the left to the left side, one will immediately[118] play two *reveses* to that side, and then turn to take the left foot and place it in front of the right, playing with it a *tajo* that ends with the point to those of said side. Then let the right foot go with the two *reveses* made immediately,[119] and return to new steps like the past ones, and take note that because the foot is lifted and placed in front of the other, and due to that there is room, so that lifting the other one will reach more to the opponents of that side, and more so as it goes gaining ground.

How to Withdraw
Having to withdraw, it is enough with the feet back wide.

f.87 **Fifth Rule: Against Being Surrounded, and Defense of One Who Plays Them**

The two swords being surrounded, throw a *tajo* in a wheel, arming the wheel on the left foot, and finish it with the same foot ending directly to the other side, in a manner that if your face was to one side when you committed the *tajo*, it will be to rear when finishing the *tajo*. Then throw another *tajo* in a wheel, arming on the right foot, with the left foot ending in front in a manner that the face ends up toward the other side, as said above. In this manner, you will go with this step, playing two, three, or four *tajos*, however many will be necessary for the space that the opponents will enclose. The *tajos* finished, the left arm leaves with a *reves*, and then turn with the same *tajos* in the manner above to that place where you had left, keeping to the step in all.

Note that when it says that you put the foot in front, it's not one in front of the other, like one who walks facing forward, but here we call *forward* that place where it goes. Make a step sideways (which we call *forward*), and when one turns, the legs have to be straight from each other, and the turn of the body is always straight, the face to one side then the other. With this same rule, you can arm three *reveses* in place of three *tajos*, and a *tajo* at the end in place of the *reves*, in a manner that if it is started with *reveses*, it will be finished with a *tajo*, and if it is started with *tajos*, it will be finished with a *reves*.

Take note that when you do a similar rule being surrounded, that you shouldn't use any thrust — save that if the opponents will squeeze you so much that it is necessary to rip them. So that you cannot be surrounded in such occasion, going ripping, arm a thrust to those that will be closer and rip with a *tajo* and *reves* with much speed.

Sixth Rule: Attacked in Front and Behind in a Wide Street f.88

When your opponents attack you in front and in back, place yourself with them to your sides,[120] the feet and legs wide, and throw to those on the right side a *reves* with the left arm and a *tajo* with the right arm, without moving the feet. The *reves* ends with a nails-down punching thrust to those on the left side. Then play a *reves* with the right arm and a *tajo* with the left arm to those on the left side. At the same time to those on the right side, give a nails-down punching thrust with the right arm that played the *reves*. Continuing this step, these thrusts always have to leave from the arm that plays the *reveses*. Note that these blows of *tajo* and *reves* have to be very long, as they start at the opponents on one side and cut to the opponents on the other side. With this step, you will battle as much as will be necessary.

The Same of Another Kind
How this rule will be done in another manner.

If he wants, or if the opponents press in, one can arm the *reves* on the left foot, giving a turn in the mode of the fifth rule, then *tajo* and turn another *reves* and *tajo* on the same left foot in a manner that to one side and the other, arming on the left foot, one plays *tajos* and *reveses*. To wit: two *reveses* and one *tajo*, and the *reves* leaving from below the arm has to cut the middle of the body and return with another, rounding above the head, offending in the high parts, and the *tajo* will always leave passing the first *reves* in a manner that it always goes between them.

Take note that if there are more opponents than one can otherwise handle with this rule, one quickly uses the rule of being surrounded. If any side retreats, use the rule against those only in front. Note

Seventh Rule: Guarding a Lady f.89

First, take note that none of the blows that this rule deals with have to pass behind, being rounded above the head, but are all armed above it, in front of the face.

Put the lady or friend that you have to defend behind your back with their head down, so that it doesn't pass above nor come equal to yours. Then throw two *reveses* with the right arm, one rounded behind the other, and then one left *reves*, and behind it another right *reves*, and a nails-down punching thrust with the left arm. Then [make] another step of two *reveses* with the left arm, rounded like those of the right arm, and behind those, a *reves* with the right arm, a *reves* with the left sword, and a nails-down punching thrust with the right arm, and a *reves* with the left arm. These two steps made, in this same form you will begin those which will be necessary for the battle.

this can be helped by Rule Eight

Step

Note that in the step of the feet that is made in this rule, the right has to always be in front, and the left behind it.

Eighth Rule: Note This Rule Can Be Done When the Opponents Surround You When Escorting the Lady

When you will battle, if you carry the cloak and want to guard it at the same time as battling, or if you carry an abundance of goods, like a load of merchandise or a valuable thing, place that thing on the floor.

Guarding a Cloak and Goods

If it is a thing that the foot and leg can turn around with three or four steps, bring the left foot near to it, and if it is a person, he will sit down. The left foot close, put the sword of the left arm below the right arm, and play a *tajo,* letting out the right foot as much as you are able. The moment the *tajo* cuts, lift the left foot and place it more in front, near what is guarded, letting out the step as much as you are able. Then make another *tajo*, putting the right foot to the side of the opponents so that it reaches, and the left more in front, near to that which is guarded, in a manner that the foot and leg that go on the outside have to be extended to the opponents, and that which goes on the inside goes near to that which is guarded, so that it will be possible with three steps to give a turn in a wheel all around that which is guarded, whether cloak, goods, or woman.

f.90

Woman

If it is a woman, she has to be seated, and giving a round of *tajos*, at the last, the left hand leaves with a *reves*, and at the same time the right foot and arm turn with another *reves*, all in one step. The right foot remaining near to that which is guarded, and the left outside, play another three *reveses*, moving the feet in the form and step above, and give another turn with *reveses* around the thing that is guarded. At the last, the right arm plays a *tajo* (note that with the previous *reveses*, the same right arm has to play them).

The *tajo* played, the left arm plays a *reves* rounded above the head, or two if it will be necessary. Turning the left foot backward, placing it near to the thing that is guarded, and with the right on the outside, begin another new step of *tajos* like the first ones. Finish like it was said in the first step and start the second. With these steps, give battle as much as necessary.

Note that as soon as one sword battles, the other has to be below the arm.

Another Rule of Guarding the Cloak

Standing to the side with the right foot on the cloak, throw a *reves* to the left side, and passing the right foot to the same left side, play a *tajo* with the right arm. Then, either make a *reves* with the left arm to that place where it left, or at the end of the same *reves*, give a nails-down punching thrust with the same sword, in a manner that when giving this *reves* and thrust, it has to be with the back turned to where he had f.91 the face when he started the rule.

When he gives the turn, he has to be armed on the left foot and then turn on the same left foot with a *reves* with the right arm, a *tajo* with the left arm, a *reves* with the right arm, and with the same right arm, a nails-down punching thrust to the same side. These two steps made, return to do the first as dealt with above, and then the second, as many times as sufficient for the battle.

This rule doesn't work for goods

Note that when playing the *tajo*, the sword has to end below the other arm.

Ninth Rule: Four Streets

If attacked by opponents in four streets, arm yourself nails-down with the swords and the arms open. Manipulating the body as much as you are able, standing firm and bending the knees, play a *tajo* and *reves* in a manner that if possible, these two blows surround the whole body, and then like this, from standing firm, another *tajo* and *reves* in the same manner as those from above. Turning in a continuous motion on the left foot, leave with a *reves*, giving a jump to one of the corners. Stopping, arm another two steps like those above. Note that when you are established on the left foot so that you will leave with a *reves*, the *reves* has to be with the right arm, and when you leave with a *reves* with the left arm, you have to be established on the right foot. Each step is made like I say: with two *reveses* and two *tajos* standing firm, leave with the *reves* turned above the head, and while falling with the jump, quickly arm the step of the two *reveses* and two *tajos*, taking one of the corners at each jump. If it will be necessary to give a jump in the middle of the street, do it; it is not bad, because the opponents do not press themselves together in a short and tight ring, but it is best of all to do one of the jumps of the step to gain one of the streets, and then do the rule that suits.

f.92 **Tenth Rule: Separating a Fight**

When it will be necessary to come to break up a fight, take note that the blows that one plays are all armed and played above the head, and on no occasion is there a thrust, so that in the brawl, it doesn't run into anyone, nor are the *tajos*, and *reveses* low so that they hit anyone, only flown above the head, intending to place yourself in the middle. Being armed on one of the feet, go to one side in a continuous motion, giving leaps with the feet while playing *reveses*. Turning in the same manner with the same *reveses* with a single sword, but when giving the turn, at the time that he turns, he plays a *tajo* and *reves* with both the swords until he turns to part. Not wanting to start off with *reveses*, start off with *tajos*, but in said manner. The sword that isn't cutting goes withdrawn below the arm of the other the moment it's not cutting. Take note that more resistance is given to the side that is stronger.

Rule Eleven: Withdrawing[121]

The swords taken by the above order, make a step from one side to the other, namely to those of the left side, and to those of the right side, never turning the back to one side or the other, but the body always straight, [and] play on one side, taking the feet to one side, one behind another, throwing a *reves* with the left arm and a *tajo* with the right arm to those on the right side. The *reves* ends with a nails-down punching thrust to those that remain on the left side, and the sword of the *tajo* ends below the left arm.

Then going with said step to those on the left side, throw a *reves* with the right arm and a *tajo* with the left arm. The *reves* finishes with a nails-down punching thrust to the same on the right side, and the sword in the left hand ends below the right arm. With this step, go to said side as much as necessary, and running them all, turn with the f.93
same step and blows to those on the other right side, keeping to the rule of the step and blows to one side and to another, as long as the fight and posture will last.

Rule Twelve: Surrounded in a Hall or Street

Taking the swords as said, turn the face to one side, and throw a *reves* with the left arm and a *tajo* with the right arm to those that will be to the right side. Those two blows have to turn over the left foot when they cut, carrying the right through the air in a wheel so that the face turns to the other side, ending where the back was. At the end of the turn, the left arm that had played the *reves* has to end at the same time with a nails-down punching thrust to those same ones on the right side where it had started. Then arm another technique of *reves* over the right foot for those on the left side, and *tajo* with left arm. Those two blows have to cut until turning the face to the other side, finishing the blow of *reves* with a nails-down punching thrust to those same ones on the left side.

Take note that these turns have to be rounded, the face ending one time to one side, and the other time to the other side. With this step, one will be able to turn to the side where he had started, and then to the other, as much as necessary.

Rule Thirteen: Guarding a Cloak, In Summary

This rule can be used in guarding a cloak, making only one step to one side, another to the other. The players of two swords should note that when they are doing a rule for one thing, if the opponents change, then the rule has to change.

PART FIVE: SWORD AND DAGGER

First Chapter on Sword and Dagger

f.94

The French posture

He that plays this weapon against another dagger takes note that all his play is outside, because of the danger that exists with the daggers being close.

How one has different techniques[122] against dagger or shield;

the dagger is offensive and defensive

When against a shield or buckler, one can choose that which suits him, choosing the inside or outside play, making use of both; one can take *tajos* or *reveses* on the sword, entering to wound with the dagger.

Slipping in and entering are the same

Take note that against two swords, one can play the game of inside and outside very well; take the *tajos* and *reveses* high on the dagger and slip in below, as will be declared in the chapters ahead. One doesn't want to make flourishes with a dagger, but to be very strong and firm in whichever posture that he will be armed, responding to the opponent's blows with much notice, and the same in the attacks.

Second Chapter

Established, one of them puts his sword nails-up with the arm in front of the belly and the dagger crossed above the head. If the opponent commits a nails-up thrust to the chest, one defends it by beating it with the dagger to his right side and giving a nails-up thrust in the chest, or one can give a deflection with the dagger, beating the sword to the floor so that it presses to his own left side, and give the same nails-up thrust in the belly. When they beat the thrust with the dagger to the floor, the opponent frees above and gives the same nails-up thrust in the face.

Third Chapter

Established nails-up, one of them places the dagger above the right shoulder. If the opponent tests the sword, consent. If he commits a nails-up thrust to the eyes, and the sword with the dagger to the outside, and without a change of feet, give a nails-up thrust in the belly. As to the dagger that is said to be placed above the shoulder, it will be better below the shoulder, close to the crook of the elbow.

f.95

Chapter Four

Established nails-up, if the opponent tests your sword, free and give a nails-up thrust on the outside in the right shoulder, which one can deflect with the dagger to his right side and give a nails-up thrust in the belly, not entering more than enough that the thrust reaches. When committing this thrust, take note that the sword has to withdraw so that it does not meet with the opponent's.

Chapter Five

Established nails-up with the daggers close to the swords, straight to the opponent, if one of them wants to lower the sword, he leaves his dagger as he had it. If the opponent travels to thrust nails-up to the chest, deflect it with the dagger and give a *reves* rounded over the head, into his head. The opponent can take this *reves* on the dagger with the point to the sky and give a nails-up thrust in the belly — instead of deflecting and giving a *reves* as said above, the opponent can press his sword on it and descend with a nails-up thrust to the thigh, taking his dagger joined to the other's sword.

Chapter Six

Established as it says in Chapter Five, when the opponent commits the nails-up thrust, gain the opponent's sword on your dagger below, and lifting it above the head, give a nails-up thrust in the thigh at the same time, not entering, only bending the body. If the opponent attacks you to the open left side, turn to undo the blow with the dagger, continuing the same thrust.

Chapter Seven

Established nails-up with the dagger and sword together, test the opponent's sword. If he leaves with a *reves* to your head before you travel with a nails-up thrust, or after the thrust is committed, if he rips it with the shield[123] and leaves with the same *reves*, quickly parry with the dagger on the right side where the *reves* travels, with the point of the dagger in the air as above, putting in the foot somewhat, and give a nails-down thrust in the belly.

Chapter Eight f.96

Established nails-up, if one of them drops the sword, the other may commit a nails-up thrust. If the opponent travels to thrust nails-up by the same edges, turn your thrust to nails-down, rotating the hand with the wrist (in a manner that the swords do not meet) and give a nails-down thrust in the belly, beating the opponent's sword over your right side with the dagger. The opponent can withdraw the foot and body backwards and give a nails-up thrust in the eyes.

Chapter Nine

Established as said above with nails-up, after said nails-up thrust is committed by the edges, the opponent can, with his dagger, gain the sword that runs with said thrust by the edges, by putting the dagger between the swords, pressing it to his left side, and giving a nails-up thrust in the chest, not entering more than enough so that said thrust reaches. This can be defended by ripping it with the dagger to the right side and giving a ripped *reves* above the head, in the opponent's head.

Chapter Ten

Established nails-up, with the daggers with the points over the wrist, if the opponent comes with a nails-up thrust to the chest, leave the dagger and defend it by the same edge nails-up thrust to the eyes. If the opponent presses your sword to his left side, quickly leave with a *reves*. Take this *reves* on the sword, and it has barely arrived when you will exchange the hands, giving the dagger to the place to where the sword was, and dropping the sword with a *reves* to the legs, withdrawing quickly.

Chapter Eleven

Established nails-down, with the dagger the same and in the same height, if the opponent tests, defend with a *reves* before it arrives to test. If this *reves* goes to the legs, take the parry with a nails-down thrust in the thigh. If the opponent lifts with a nails-up thrust to the chest, deflect it with the dagger and give a ripped *reves* above the head to the same legs. If the opponent guards the legs and goes with the same nails-up thrust to the chest, deflect it with a ripped *tajo* from the f.97
head to the knees.

Note that the *reves* is deflected with the dagger, and the *tajo* with the sword. Take note that in these deflections of the dagger putting in the parry that suits the opponent's blow.

Chapter Twelve

Wherever established nails-down as said above, if the opponent commits a nails-up throwing[124] thrust to the chest, quickly beat it with the dagger to your right side and give a nails-up or nails-down thrust in the belly, entering only enough so that you reach. When he comes with the same throwing[125] thrust, you can also free below and give a nails-up thrust in the shoulder, beating the sword to his left side, or rip it with a *tajo* to the side below the arm. This *tajo* can be taken on the dagger before it lowers, giving a nails-up thrust in the thigh. Against this, the opponent can withdraw the leg a little bit and give a nails-up thrust in the eyes. Note that all these techniques have to be played outside, and the dagger waiting for the blows in the way, because there is no trick in those.[126]

Chapter Thirteen

Whenever one is established in whatever posture that you may be when the opponent puts in a foot to give a thrust or *reves*, the foot and leg will be withdrawn where said blows go, and at the same time you will give a nails-up thrust in the chest below the shield,[127] or a *tajo* in the same sword arm. This blow is not bad if you look at it carefully.

Chapter Fourteen

Coming to cross, if one descends with a *reves* to the legs, the same will be used. Not wanting to attend to the parry with the sword or with the dagger, one can guard the leg enough that the blow passes and give a *reves* in the sword arm at the time that he goes descending with his blow. Not wanting to keep to the rule of the *reves* to the arm, one can give a *tajo* in the side below the dagger arm, taking the opponent's blows with his dagger.

f.98 ## Chapter Fifteen

Established nails-up, if one lowers the sword in a low posture, the opponent may commit a nails-up thrust to the thigh. If the one who lowered withdraws the leg and commits a nails-up thrust to the eyes, lift quickly and cross, then lower with a *reves*, giving the dagger to the opponent's sword; this *reves* has to be retreating. When you retreat, if the opponent commits a nails-up thrust, gain his sword in the middle with yours and run a nails-up thrust to the eyes. Note that this technique[128] requires speed.

Chapter Sixteen

One can use this same rule the second that the opponent gains his sword, crossing to gain it with his dagger, and give a nails-down or nails-up thrust in the belly. When said nails-up thrust is committed, the opponent can gain it with the sword, pressing it to his left side, and give a *reves* in the face without putting in the foot, and the dagger will remain in the place where the sword leaves, but at the point.

Chapter Seventeen: Enchained

Established nails-up with the dagger over the right arm, if the opponent tests, consent, and after testing, if he comes with a nails-up thrust to the eyes, enchain[129] him. How one enchains is that when the Ch. 34
opponent comes with the thrust, you exchange the arms, passing the dagger arm to the right side, and the sword gives the nails-up thrust in the opponent's right shoulder, and the moment said thrust goes, return the left arm to its side, pressing on the opponent's sword that is now locked between your dagger and sword.

Chapter Eighteen

When the opponent enchains, the opponent can free with a *reves* to the leg, which is defended by giving a nails-down thrust in the thigh, leaving the dagger in reserve. If the opponent turns with a *tajo* to the head, take the blow on the dagger and give a nails-up thrust in the belly, taking note that these similar thrusts are not inside. If the opponent doesn't free with a *reves*, but with a *tajo*, take the *tajo* on f.99
the sword, because in this time it is better than on the dagger. Taken, leave with a high *tajo*, taking note of the blows and counters of the opponent, giving the parry that is necessary to each.

Chapter Nineteen: How One Takes the Parries with the Dagger

The dagger has no obligation to take the parries in the same manner, as many practice, but to give the dagger to the blow in agreement with the manner that proceeds: If the *tajo* or *reves* comes from high to low, the dagger is placed crossed, and if it comes from the side in the mode of a slap, the dagger is placed with the point straight to the sky in that place to where the blow goes. If it will be a *tajo*, one loads the dagger to his left side, and if it will be with a *reves*, he loads it to the right side, which is not necessary when the *tajo* or *reves* comes from high to low. In the blows that will go to the legs, one will take the parries with the point toward the floor.

Chapter Twenty

After having enchained, or going to enchain, if the opponent leaves with a *reves* to the head, take note that the parry has to be with the sword, then descending with a *reves* to the legs, placing the dagger where the sword had left, as already dealt with before.

Chapter Twenty-One: Enchained

One can enchain, being established nails-up with the sword somewhat low, the point of the sword loaded to the left side, and the dagger on the right side, established above the sword. If the opponent commits a nails-up thrust to the chest or eyes against this posture, exchange the hands (as dealt with in Chapter Seventeen) and enchain, taking note of the counters as dealt with in Chapters Eighteen and Nineteen, giving the remedy contained in them. After enchaining, you can retreat, cutting *tajo* and *reves*.

f.100

Chapter Twenty-Two

After established in whatever posture that one may be, throw a false *tajo* that passes in vain. If the opponent commits a nails-up thrust, one can enchain in the mode of Chapter Seventeen, taking note of the counters of Chapters Eighteen and Nineteen. When you don't want to defend said nails-up thrust by enchaining, it can be defended in the same mode declared before.

Chapter Twenty-Three

Established in whatever posture that one may be, if the opponent throws a *tajo* to your head, throw another to his legs. Take note that when you throw a *tajo* to the legs, the opponent has to throw a *tajo* to your head because it remains uncovered, which you will take on the dagger in the mode that Chapter Nineteen deals with, and give a *reves* in the legs. At the beginning, if the opponent started with a *reves* and not with a *tajo*, start with a *reves*, and if the opponent loads with a *reves* to the head, take the parry on the dagger how it is said, passing the dagger to the right shoulder with the point to the sky and, withdrawing the right arm as much as you can, give a *tajo* in the legs, retreating.

Chapter Twenty-Four

Established nails-up, if one of them tests the sword, free quickly below and give a nails-up thrust in the right shoulder. If the opponent defends that thrust by gaining it with his dagger on the inside and pressing it on the same left side, giving a nails-up thrust in the thigh or a *reves* to the legs, take the foot back with a *reves* to his sword arm, retreating backwards.

Chapter Twenty-Five

Established nails-up with the daggers nails-up in the same position as the sword, if the opponent tests your sword, consent. If he gives a nails-up thrust to the chest, deflect to your right side and give a nails-down thrust in the belly. If the opponent deflects this thrust with a f.101
reves or with a *tajo*, quickly free it and parry on the dagger (as dealt with in Chapter Nineteen), giving a nails-up thrust in place of the nails-down thrust.

The opponent can take note that when he goes to deflect, if the opponent freed, he has to give the same thrust as before, because no one has ever ripped such that, when he frees it, he doesn't return with the same thrust. Because of that, if he rips one, he is obligated to rip the second.

Chapter Twenty-Six

Established in whatever manner that one may be, if the opponent throws a long *reves*, retreat and throw another in the same tone. If they continue ripped *reveses* above the head, they continue withdrawing the right foot, putting it in, and placing the daggers to the right side all the times that the *reveses* pass, in the manner of parrying the head and face. Running said *reveses* from side to side, when the opponent's sword passes, you can put yourself in with the same *reves*, and give it in the legs, parrying the opponent's *reves* that comes. One has this same manner when giving a nails-up thrust in place of the *reves* to the legs that is said above. When the *reves* goes above the head in order to descend, turn the hand at the wrist with a nails-up thrust to the eyes, or give a *tajo* in the head from that same place, turning the *tajo* from the wrist. Note that when this *tajo*, *reves*, or thrust is given, the opponent passes the dagger to the right side, taking the parry to your *reves*, thinking that it is truly committed, and he is uncovered on the left side in this manner.

Chapter Twenty-Seven

Keeping to the same rule from Chapter Twenty-Six, they can give those three blows of *tajo*, *reves*, and thrust in the low parts, but instead of those of said chapter that originate from over the head when the
f.102 sword wants to descend, give those below when your sword starts to rise, in a manner that you stop raising said *reves* that goes ripping and turn with a *tajo* to the leg, continuing your dagger to parry the opponent's *reves* that goes. You can give the same *tajo* in the sword arm, or you can give a nails-up thrust in the belly, not putting yourself in more than enough that it reaches.

Chapter Twenty-Eight

Established nails-up with the points of the swords to the floor, one gains the opponent's sword below, pressing it to his left side, and gives a *reves* in the right leg. When they give said *reves,* the opponent can take the leg back such that [the blow] passes by and give a *tajo* in the legs, which the opponent can defend by taking it on the dagger with the point to the floor. If the opponent turns with a *reves* to the other side to the lower parts, defend with a nails-down thrust to the thigh. If he goes with a *reves* to the head, take the blow on the dagger, with a nails-up thrust to the thigh, not entering.

Chapter Twenty-Nine

Established nails-up, if the opponent joins your sword to gain and press it to your left side, leave by the point of his sword with a *reves* to the face, running by the edges of his sword, and as you leave to the point of his sword, gain it with your dagger. This *reves* can be defended by taking it with the dagger in parry and giving a nails-up thrust in the thigh; since the opponent has gained it as said above, one can free it below. If the opponent doesn't gain your sword to the left side as in the beginning, but to the right side, leave by the point with a *tajo* to the face, running your sword by the edges of the opponent's.

This *tajo* is defended by taking the parry on the dagger and giving a *reves* in the legs.

Chapter Thirty

Established nails-up with their daggers armed at the eyes, if the opponent throws a blow below the arm to the elbow, turn the elbow to the sky so that the opponent's sword passes in vain and give a nails- f.103
down thrust in the chest. The opponent can defend this thrust by deflecting it to the right side with the dagger and giving a nails-down thrust in the belly, which can be defended by his opponent by gaining it with his sword above, pressing it to his right side. The opponent can free above and give the nails-up thrust in the same place. He that will play sword and dagger takes note that whenever the opponent undoes a thrust, gaining it as it says above, that in having to free, one has to return with the same thrust to where they had gained the other.

Chapter Thirty-One: Against Sword Alone

When you will battle against one who wields only a sword, take note that it is much better to take the opponent's blows on the sword than on the dagger, because they will be taken with more surety, and at the same time, wound with the dagger in the parts that the opponent uncovers.

Chapter Thirty-Two

The chapter before dealt with what to do against one wielding only a sword, taking the *tajos* and *reveses* only on the sword. One makes use of the same rule when the opponent throws thrusts, which you can defend by pressing on them to one side or the other and at the same time entering and offending with the dagger. No more or less to the blows that go to the legs, whether *tajo* or *reves*, attending to it with the sword to parry and wounding with the dagger.

Chapter Thirty-Three

One can keep the same order when the dagger wielder encounters one who wields a shield, buckler, or cloak in battle, taking their blows on the sword and wounding with the dagger. Of course they could take them on the dagger and wound with the sword, but taking them on the sword is the safer case.

Note

f.104 But the shield, buckler, or cloak-wielder, having to battle a dagger wielder, in my advice, should avoid the blows of *tajo* and *reves,* because of the danger of the dagger wielder parrying them on the sword and entering to wounding him with his dagger, without being able to be stopped.

Chapter Thirty-Four: Enchained

Established in whatever posture that one may be whenever the opponent gives the chest uncovered to you, commit a nails-up thrust. If the opponent enchains it as dealt with in Chapter Seventeen and associated, turn the thrust (that you had committed nails-up) to nails-down before the chain is locked. When you give said thrust, press on the opponent's sword, so that it is safer, and this nails-down thrust has to be given in the thigh.

The counters go ahead Or, when they enchain you, free above the point of the dagger with the wrist and give a nails-up thrust in the eyes, not lifting the arm, only twisting the wrist, or dropping the same nails-up thrust to the thigh.

Chapter Thirty-Five: Against Enchained

When the opponent frees with a nails-up thrust to the eyes, he that enchains can deflect it to his right side with the dagger and give a nails-down thrust in the thigh, and the two that go low to the thigh, beat them with the dagger on the right side and offer to the opponent the blow of thrust, *tajo*, or *reves*, wherever he sees the opponent more uncovered. And yet he that is enchained, if he takes note quickly, can give a nails-up thrust in the chest, eyes, or belly, or a *tajo* in the head, which is taken on the dagger as in Chapter Nineteen, giving a *reves*, leaving outside.

Chapter Thirty-Six: Enchained

They can defend the two thrusts that go to the thigh, taking them with the sword crossed low; having crossed, turning nails-up below the opponent's sword, give a nails-up thrust in the thigh. That which goes to the belly can be defended in the same tone, crossing low with his f.105
sword; having crossed, the opponent's thrust being undone, turn nails-up below and give the thrust in the belly.

Chapter Thirty-Seven

The two standing in posture, one of them nails-down with the dagger nails-down, the arms open — if the opponent comes with a nails-up thrust to the chest, suddenly do two things: Beat the opponent's sword that comes with the thrust to your right side, and at the same time give a *tajo* in the shins.

Note that one and the other have to be at one time, which is no more than an exchange of arms, and this *tajo* has to be entering somewhat. When the technique[130] is finished, you are left with the arms crossed.

Enchained
If the opponent commits a nails-up thrust to the eyes, you can enchain it in said form, or gain the opponent's sword with your dagger, press it to the left side, and give a nails-up thrust in the thigh, or rip it with a ripped *reves* to the head.

Chapter Thirty-Eight

Established nails-up, the dagger positioned in front of the chest, or established nails-down at the same height, if the opponent commits a nails-up thrust to the chest, gain his sword with your dagger [from] below, lifting it above the head, uncovering the left side well, and give a nails-up thrust in the thigh from outside. If the opponent lowers with a nails-up thrust to the uncovered left side, turn the dagger with the point to the floor, undoing it, and give a nails-up thrust in the eyes. You will do the same as we say if the opponent commits a *tajo* to the left side.

Chapter Thirty-Nine

Established nails-up, if the opponent tests your sword, free and give a nails-up thrust in the right shoulder from the outside. The opponent can deflect this thrust to the right side with the dagger and give
f.106 another nails-up thrust in the opponent's same right shoulder, which is naturally given in the eyes.

Chapter Forty: Enchained

Whenever the opponent commits a ripped *tajo*, you can take this *tajo* by crossing your sword and your dagger in the air, taking the blow in that cross, and exchange the hands quickly, enchaining in the mode of Chapter Seventeen, giving the counters and re-counters in the mode of Chapter Thirty-Five and associated chapters. The same *tajo* can be enchained without doing the same cross, taking the *tajo* only on the dagger, sneaking the sword below, directing the thrust (this has to be done quickly). The same can enchain a *reves*, taking the *reves* on the dagger, and at the same time directing the thrust below in order to enchain with all possible speed.

Chapter Forty-One: Enchained

When by chance both are enchained at the same time, one of them frees his sword by the point of the opponent's dagger and drops the sword in the place where it had enchained. If the opponent will not enchain with it and gives the thrust, leave cutting with a *tajo* and *reves*.

Chapter Forty-Two

Established nails-up, or in whatever manner that one may be, if the opponent gives a nails-up thrust to the chest, you can beat it with your dagger to the right side and give a *tajo* in the elbow at the same time. If the opponent comes with another nails-up thrust to the chest that remains uncovered at the time that you give the *tajo* in the elbow, gain his sword with your dagger, pressing it to the left side, and give a nails-up thrust in the thigh, leaving with *tajo* and *reves*.

Chapter Forty-Three: Enchained

f.107

Establish yourself nails-up with the dagger across the chest. If the opponent commits a nails-up thrust, enchain in the mode said in Chapter Seventeen and associated. You can do the same when you are established, if the opponent tests and comes with a nails-up thrust to the chest. You will do the same if the opponent establishes himself and doesn't want to leave; test his sword, and if the opponent leaves with a nails-up thrust to the chest, enchain. One who prides himself on enchaining doesn't have to put the dagger in a known place, but hidden from the opponent's view and, having time and place, moving with speed.

Chapter Forty-Four

Whenever the opponent throws a *reves* to your head, take the parry on the dagger and give a *reves* in the sword arm with the wrist. You will take the same into account when the opponent begins the *reves*, giving a touch in the arm outside and withdrawing, and if he goes with a *tajo*, giving the blow with a *tajo* in the sword arm and withdrawing, or giving a nails-up thrust to the eyes.

Chapter Forty-Five

Established nails-up, place your sword low, in front of the belly, and the dagger close to the chest. If the opponent commits a nails-up thrust to the chest, gain his sword with your dagger from below, lifting it high, and give a thrust below the armpit of the sword arm, which serves against someone armored, because the armor never reaches to such place.

Armored
This thrust can be defended by freeing the sword from the power of the dagger, gaining the opponent's sword with much speed from inside to outside to the right side, and at the same time giving a nails-down thrust in the thigh – or lifting the sword arm and, beating it with the dagger at the same time, giving a ripped *reves* in the head.

f.108

Chapter Forty-Six

In dealing with the enchained before, I say that in all the techniques[131] — thrust, *tajo*, *reves* — one can enchain, keeping to the rule of enchaining as was declared before. Being the case that you can enchain by running your sword along the opponent's arm in place of his sword, do it, because it makes two wounds: One on the arm, the other the thrust.

Chapter Forty-Seven

When they go to enchain, he that feels himself enchained, before the chain is perfect, can turn the sword nails-down between the opponent's sword and dagger. Note that it has to be with much speed, because when the dagger enchains, if it is united, you will not be able to remedy yourself afterward.

Chapter Forty-Eight: How Chapter Forty Five of the Shield Has to Be Used in This Rule

The rule of the shield from Chapter Forty-Five, folio eighty, can be used with the dagger, which, as a general rule, the double weapon will be used as the dagger, keeping in all to the rule of the dagger, in its parries and attacks.

Chapter Forty-Nine

Established nails-up, give a blow below the opponent's arm, swaying back. If the opponent continues a nails-up thrust to the chest, quickly gain his sword from below with the dagger and give him a nails-up thrust in the belly without entering, so that he arrives to your sword with the force with which he had left.

Chapter Fifty: How the Cloak Will Be Taken with the Dagger

He that will come with cloak at the time of the battle, carrying his dagger (which will go on the left side and not the right as Chapter Fifty One deals with), can ready the cloak at the same time very well, in a manner that it remains fallen on the arm behind the hilt, keeping to the rule of cloak and sword in Chapter Two.

Chapter Fifty-One: Declaration in Summary on Things Particular to the Dagger f.109

In general, he that will battle against shield, buckler, or cloak with sword and dagger can rip with *tajo* and *reves* to the end that the opponent is disarmed. As bad as the ripping play is for them, it is good for the dagger wielder, because the best that the dagger wielder can have from the opponent is to rip him, or simply to play *tajos* or *reveses*.

Shieldman Note

Note that it has to be with the condition that the opponent's ripped *tajos* have to be parried on the sword, and not the dagger, as declared in its place, that if it had been necessary to take them on the dagger, it's not bad for the shieldman or buckler-man to rip; because of that, when the shieldman or buckler-man will meet with the dagger and the party skilled in its use, the best choice is being established and playing the nails-up thrusts from outside, seeking speed in freeing.

How to Carry the Dagger on the Waist

As far as he that carries the dagger on the waist, it seems that they carry it these days more for bravery and pride than as a defensive and offensive weapon, carrying it on the right side because the sword is seen on one side and the dagger on the other, and in this manner they enclose the sides, fortified like armored walls, and not like a body harnessed with weapons. The dagger should be carried on the same side as the sword, and not over the quillons of it, putting it in front as some carry it, so it is seen – all the more so if trimmed with gold. Furthermore, carrying on the left side means carrying it in the middle of the back (on the waistline), because in that place, it is gripped with more ease than in any other place. On the right side, to draw the sword and dagger, the hands remain crossed, and at the drawing and uncrossing, the arms can be cut. In addition, the dagger has to be carried hidden from sight.

PART SIX: THE TWO-HANDED SWORD

First Chapter on the Montante and Declarations About It f.110

How the Montante Has to Be Carried, and How It Has to Be Held

There are many obligations a person must keep when handling and battling with a *montante*. We see in battles that many come to lose by lacking these methods; neither from dropping it from being badly wounded, nor from perhaps tripping and falling, nor from other unfortunate events that a man cannot resist, but by being over-taken by opponents armed with only a sword, and others with a sword and shield. I have seen an opponent with sword and dagger, after having his sword broken, gain the *montante* with only the dagger. It was and is the reason why, in place of true rules, they make flourishes, which are necessary only for masters, while the rules for the players are as follows.

For he that will learn the *montante* in order to defend his person and injure his enemy or enemies, does its rules at the time of battle with much sense and caution, making each one in its necessary place (which is why they are called "rules"); for instance, he does not do the withdrawing rule when surrounded, nor the surrounded rule when having opponents in front, nor with too much speed, except when pressed. If you would strike advantageously, do your rule with heavy and measured step, and not like those who dance. Nor is there a place for too much speed. Note

If you leave at night, carry the *montante* without a sheath, or at least with the sheath removed. When you will hold of the *montante* in the beginning of the battle, the fingers don't have to pass out to the thirds.[132] Adhere to the other conditions previously mentioned in this chapter. Be sure that the cloak, hat, or sheath doesn't remain in the street, so that no one comes to know of the person who has been there. Because of that, I suggest that at night, the *montante* is carried without a sheath, and the wielder without a cloak, and the *montante* in the left hand, tilted diagonally, and not on the back as many carry it.[133] Note f.111

Two Montantes

When one has a battle against another *montante*, one should not make use of rules, but of established battle (as two swords), being defended and injuring with thrusts. In no case are *tajos* or *reveses* played (which is counter to many opinions), because in doing them, there will not fail to be great trouble; they will only be established in the middle of the body, testing or not testing. The thrusts that have to be committed or defended on the right side have to be nails-down, and those on the left side nails-up, keeping in all to the general rule of the first chapter of single sword, folio 12.[134]

Second Chapter: Surrounded in a Very Narrow Street

When in a narrow street, surrounded on both sides, if it will be such that you cannot play *tajos* or *reveses* in it, put your back against one of those walls. Turning the *montante* at the wrist so that it is above the crook of the left elbow of the left arm, which remains withdrawn to the chest, put the right foot to the left side with much speed, and at the same time extend the arms, giving a nails-up thrust to those on that side. Just as the thrust is given with the foot put in and the back against the other wall, turn the point of the *montante* in the air, bending at the wrist, above the left arm. In the manner given above, put in the right foot with a nails-up thrust to those on the right side, ending
f.112 with your back on the other wall, in a manner that putting in the foot, withdrawing the thrust, placing the *montante* above the arm, and committing the thrust all have to be made in one step and one time.

If it is necessary to retreat, when you put in the foot and leg, put it in suddenly, giving a jump to the side to which you have to leave, which should be the side where you see more weakness. Do this step continually until retreating, and to those on the other side, put in the foot and leg with the ordinary step, only using it for as long as the battle lasts. This rule is practiced in a continuous motion, giving the thrusts, and certainly I want to point out the faults that it has, as they will be noticed in good judgment If a thrust is thrown to the floor, and another in the air, giving it a good beginning and bad ending, it should indeed be done by the steps and order of the beginning.

Gangway of a Galley

The same rule will be used in a gangway of a galley, the slave benches becoming the "walls" that are dealt with in the beginning of the rule, but this is understood as the opponents being in control of the stern and bow. Being at one of those, it is enough to attack them with nails-down and nails-up thrusts, whichever will cover better according to his sense, putting in the foot and taking it back.

Attacked on One Side

The same can be used in a narrow street when you are attacked on only one side of it.

Third Rule: Surrounded in a Somewhat Narrow Street from Behind and in Front, and How to Grip the Montante

If you are surrounded with opponents behind and in front in a street where *tajos* and *reveses* cannot be played, take hold of the *montante* with the right hand close to the quillons and the left close to the pommel and turn your sides to the opponents and your back to one
of the walls. Play a *tajo* to those on the right side, putting the right f.113
foot to that same side. This *tajo* has to be armed in the air and has to cut from high to low, because if the street had room for the *tajos* to be ripped in the middle of the body, the rule for being surrounded would be better. Play a *tajo* in this manner, and the *tajo* does not stop until it ends in a nails-up thrust[135] to those that are on the left side. At the same time, put to the left side the foot that you had put to the right side, from one side to the other in a manner that the body ends up turned with the back to the other wall. The placing of the foot, the *tajo*, the turn, and the armed thrust all have to be in one time.

Then turn with a *reves* to those on the same right side, which goes armed above the head in the manner of the *tajo* and finishes with a nails-down thrust to those on the left side in the manner of the nails-up thrust that is dealt with above. When the *reves* passes, put the left foot in with it in the manner that you put in the right foot in the first step, so that the body ends turned, and your back turned to the other wall. The placing of the left foot, the *reves*, the armed thrust, and the turn of the body all have to be made in one time.

Take note that when you turn the body, the step [having been] made, you have to turn your face to the opponents, that is, to where the blows began, in the manner that your eyes go after the *montante.* Continue the battle as long as necessary with the two above-mentioned steps of the left and right foot.

Fourth Rule: Against a Shieldman

Take hold of the *montante* in the manner of Chapter Three and, putting in the right foot, play a *tajo* to the legs of the shieldman. The *tajo* f.114 cuts until it turns above your head, and the *montante* ends armed for a *reves*, nails-up with the point to the floor, the quillons covering your head. Then, putting in the left foot, play a *reves* to the legs, giving a turn with the *montante* until it stops above your head with the point to the floor and the quillons covering your head. The point that ends at the floor like this has to be nails-down, because then the *tajo* is armed. With these two steps of *tajo* and *reves*, give battle as long as it will be necessary.

Note Note that the points that I make mention of in this rule are not committed thrusts,[136] just armed, so that the shieldman does not slip in below. Because of that, they are positioned toward the floor like this, and time is not wasted on them, as in order to have a *tajo* or *reves* armed, the *montante* necessarily has to be turned in that manner, making two movements. In the manner pointed out, only one movement is made.

Fifth Rule: Against Two Shieldmen

Taking hold of the *montante* in the manner of Chapter Three, and having the opponents in front, throw a *tajo* to the one on the right side, putting the right foot towards him. The *tajo* cuts until it reaches the opponent on the left side.[137] When the *tajo* cuts, the foot that you put to that side is lifted and placed in front of the left at the same time, so that you may more easily reach the opponent on the left side.

When the *tajo* cuts in the above form, it does not have to stop until it turns to a half *reves* above your head, the point of the *montante* ending nails-up at the right side enemy, toward the floor so that the opponent doesn't slip in below, and the quillons high so that they defend the head from the blow that the shieldman might play.

Note

f.115 Note that the *tajo*, including putting in the foot, placing it in front of the left, and the turn with the *tajo* until stopping in said posture, all has to be made in one single time, no more, no less. The passage of time is the same as the rule against one shieldman.

Note Note that when it says *two shieldmen*, it is understood that it's the same for more, until the street is filled.

Having made this step, put the left foot to the same side and play a *reves* that cuts through to those on the right side, lifting the left foot that and putting it in front of the right. The *reves* will not stop until it turns above the head with the point nails-down at the opponents on the same side, and the point inclined toward the floor, so that the opponent doesn't slip in below. Take note that the *reves*, the putting in and removing of the foot, and arming the point all have to be in one single time.

Note that the point that you arm nails-down necessarily has to be turned in order to arm the *reves*, which would be made in two times if not done in this form, and in the declared order, it is no more than one. Note

The turn of the blow is very necessary to arm said points, which serve to parry the blows that the opponents are able to give as soon as the *montante* passes, and the posture of the point impedes the entrance below the *montante*; this should be done quickly. Many other rules can be given, but this is not the place for them.[138] The two steps of left and right foot made, repeat as long as the battle lasts.

As well, if there were more than two shieldmen, one could cut with *tajos* to the legs and return with *reveses*, in the manner of Rule Nine, folio 118. Note

Rule Six: Guarding a Lady – and Goods

Take hold of the *montante* in the manner of Chapter Three, and have the woman or friend that you intend to keep safe attached to your belt from behind, advising them to not exert force on it, only so that they f.116 remain safely behind your back. Then play a *tajo*, putting in the right foot, and a *reves* putting in the left foot, which do not leave flying toward the rear, so as not to injure the one that is guarded; it will only come to the shoulders when it is armed. The *tajo* will not pass on the left side, however many there are, and if there are two, the *tajo* is with the wrist and will not pass on the right side. The *reves*, accordingly, will not pass on the right side, however many there are, and if there are two, it will not pass on the left side and is done with the wrist. With this step, one will battle as much as necessary.
In case there is one, it is enough to only defend with a nails-up Note thrust with the right foot, and nails-down with left foot, if he is not a shieldman. With the same thrusts, one can defend against two, also not being shieldmen. If they will surround him, he makes use of Rule

Seven ahead, sitting the person down.

Seventh Rule: To Guard Goods and Cloak

If some person is walking with an important load of goods, or in whatever manner it becomes necessary to defend an abundance of goods while being attacked by many, he places the load on the floor. Then, being as close as possible, the left foot placed next to it, launching the right foot to the side, he cuts a *tajo*, extending the arms and body as much as he can. As soon as the *tajo* runs, he lifts the left foot and puts it more in front, close to the thing he is guarding, placing the right as described in the manner above. With this step, he makes three *tajos*, with which he goes completely around the goods. When it cannot be circled with three *tajos*, he makes one more step afterward,
f.117 and at the same time another *tajo*, so that there are four steps and four *tajos*, and no more. Then he turns with a thrust in a continuous motion over the left foot, taking the right foot and placing it close to that which is guarded, as the left had been. The left is put in with a *reves*, lifting the right then and putting it more forward, close to the goods. The left sets off in front with another *reves*, launching it out as much as he can, with the body and all. With this step, he encircles his goods with three steps and three blows of *reves*, and when he cannot, there may be four, but no more. Those made, he turns, arming thrusts nails-down or -up over the right foot (as I say left), turns to put the left foot close to the goods, and does the same step and *tajos* done at the beginning. Finished, he returns with the second step of *reves* and does it as many times as necessary in the battle.

Note This rule can be done in guarding a cloak and in guarding a lady, when one will be surrounded, but make the person sit down.

Rule Eight: Guarding a Cloak[139]

The *montante* taken as dealt with in Chapter Three, put the left foot on the cloak, then bending the body and extending the arms as much as you can, play a raking[140] *tajo* to the legs. Passing the right foot to the left side so that your face ends up where you had your back, play another *tajo*, higher, in a manner that there have to be two *tajos* and one single step of the right foot, armed over the left foot. The two *tajos* given, turn to pass the right foot to the place where you had it, playing two *reveses*, one to the legs and another higher. The first blow

always has to be the lowest, in a manner that you give two *reveses* in one single step with the right foot, and the left foot doesn't leave from over the cloak. Always when you finish the last *tajo* and the last *reves*,
the *montante* encircles your back, turning your whole body in a circle f.118
while leaving the feet in place, the left over the cloak and the right always to the side of the left, and both very straight. Give battle with this step as much as necessary.

This rule isn't ruined by speed, nor are there thrusts in it.

Ninth Rule: Having People in Front in a Wide Street

The *montante* positioned in the manner said in Chapter Three, being attacked by many in front in a wide street, one begins with much speed to cut all the *tajos* that his speed will allow in the middle height to one of the sides, the left foot always traveling to the other point of the opponents, in a manner that one starts on the right side and finishes on the left. Note how I say that the left foot is that which moves, and then the right after, being placed each time in front of the left, gaining ground. As the last *tajo* arrives, the *montante* remains withdrawn in a half *tajo*, lifting the quillons close and straight to the head with the point to the floor, with the arms turned over in the manner of a *reves.*

Take note that all this has to be in one single time, and in this same time, one turns with *reveses* in the manner of the *tajos* in the middle of the body, traveling to the right side with the right foot in front and the left after, gaining ground ahead of the right. Upon reaching the last opponent's side, the last *reves* ends withdrawn in the air in the mode of the *tajo*; no more, no less. Then one begins another step with *tajos* like
the first, and another step with *reveses* like the second, and as many f.119
more as necessary for the battle, keeping in all to the order of the two steps of *tajo* and *reves* I declared.

This same rule will be done in a street that is not very wide, as one can use said *tajos* and *reveses* in it, or Rule Five against two shieldmen will be done, only that the blows can go low or high, as suits the *montante* wielder.

Tenth Rule: Surrounded in a Plaza, Field, or Street

One must have much acuity, speed, and great vigor when surrounded by opponents in a battle. One quickly takes up his *montante* by the form in Rule Three. Positioned in the middle of the attackers, he cuts a *tajo*, bending at the knees with the head straight, established on the left foot. Then he cuts another, putting in the right foot, in a manner that he goes sideways, alternating left and right foot, cutting *tajos* in a continuous motion, circling himself in a wheel with the *montante*, giving a *tajo* at each step, which may be up to three or four, and not passing five because of the danger that it can have in weakening the head. These steps with *tajos* finished, he returns to where he started with other steps with *reveses*, in the same order as the *tajos*, giving a *reves* at each step of the foot, and circling his whole body with the *reves*. Note that when you turn with said blows, the feet are placed surely, and more than this, they are always placed straight from each other, the body always going very upright, the face alternating from one side to the other. In this manner, stepping to one side with tajos, and then to the other with reveses, do these steps for as long as the
f.120 battle lasts.

Note Take note that if you will be surrounded in a wide field, that when you give the steps, they aren't always to one side, returning to where you had left, but continually stepping first to one side, then to another, running the whole circuit in a wheel.

Note If the encirclement will be in a wide street, make the steps to one side and the other. Take note that in no manner is there a thrust.[141] If it happens that you have to break the squad of enemies that keeps you surrounded, press with the step to the side where you see more weakness, and arriving close, shout with a loud voice,[142] and at the same time, give a nails-up thrust to that side with a big leap in a circle, and at the end of the thrust, a *tajo* and *reves*.

Note Being outside, take advantage of them with Rule 9. Be advised that the moment you are surrounded, that you always press to the side to where the opponents are stronger.

Rule Eleven: In a Wide Street, Attacked on Both Sides

Positioned in the middle of the street, keeping in step with Rule Ten – inasmuch as it deals with moving the feet, positioned sideways and armed on the left foot – play a *tajo* with all possible vigor, putting the right foot to the other side, and turn the left foot in a wheel with another *tajo*, not bending the body, but upright, extending the arms as much as you can. Finishing the two *tajos*, turn to those that remain on the right side and thrust nails-up. At the end of it, turn with another two steps of right and left foot, cutting two *reveses* to the side where you had started, in the form of the *tajos*, and at the end of them, turn to thrust nails-down to those that remain on the left side.

Note that these thrusts do not fall directly to the right or left side if the steps and blows are odd, because if they are like this, said thrust always falls to one side. Because of this you have to make two or four blows, and no more, because of the danger to the head (as dealt with in Rule Ten). The thrusts are very necessary because the blows of *tajo* and *reves* are armed from them. Take note that due to that, they do not have to be made in two times – to wit: *tajo* and thrust, *reves* and thrust – but at the end of the *tajo*, when it returns, finish it with said thrust. The thrust is thrown so that those opponents that pursue you as you pursue the others have to keep their distance. The thrust is allowed here because the opponents are not in a circle, but to the side. Note f.121

It is neither necessary for the person to bend, nor circle the body with the *montante*, as he doesn't have opponents in a circle; if it had been like this, it wouldn't be necessary to distinguish from Rule Ten. This is to give each thing its own place and to make nothing hidden. Note

Rule Twelve: Separating a Fight

Much sense and caution is required to break up a fight and separate the opponents, so that one does not seek to go halting injury and happen to make it greater due to many people being together in such cases. As a brawl causes carelessness, it is necessary that whoever has to separate it goes with much sense, so that after he arrives to them, he begins to clear the way, putting himself in the middle of them, going in turns, alternating from one foot to the other in jumps or hops, giving *tajos* and *reveses* above the head, and not below, because if it will be like this, one will not stop injuries – only above the head, which only

causes dread and fear in those that are present, encountering only
f.122 the swords with his *montante*, always pressing to the side that has a greater concourse of people. But with all this, the step does not stop being in the form of giving only one blow with each step of the feet, and no more, nor in any case will a thrust be played, which is very dangerous in these cases. After the middle is dominated, if he wants, one can make use of Rule Six, on guarding goods. In this rule, much speed causes harm.

Rule Thirteen: Four Streets

There are many opinions for a *montante* wielder which originates from being attacked in an intersection (in this way, two streets seem to be four). And if the battle has to be given where said streets meet, making four corners, then in my opinion, I would not do that in this place, but by Rule Ten which deals with being surrounded.

Note If I am told that the battle started in the beginning of the street, and the opponents backed off until they arrived at the four corners, and the enemies go again on each side (or only one) and will be able to injure him from the side, I say that in this case the *montante* wielder takes note that when he gives battle and they arrive to said corners, he seeks to remain in the middle of the street, so he has enough room in order to work.

Note If I am told that it is necessary to turn the corner, the same should be done to give battle until gaining all of the front of the street where the opponents are gathered. If I am told that one necessarily has to turn close to the corner, it is easy to send the *montante* in front, stitched to the wall with a thrust, extending the arms as much as he can, and then
f.123 continue the rule that will be necessary for the occasion. The rest is folly, making flourishes while a person's life hangs in the balance.

Rule Fourteen: For the Master to Make a Flourish, the Application of Which I Leave to the *Diestros*

Taking hold of the *montante* in the manner pointed out in Rule Three, and positioned sideways, move with the left foot to the same side, and play two or three *tajos*, stepping also to the side, the right foot following, being placed each time ahead of the left – I mean to say ahead as in front of the line of sight. The *tajos* played, leave the last withdrawn in the air in the form of Rule Nine, with the quillons in front of the face, the arms turned in the manner of an armed *reves*, and the point of the *montante* towards the floor. Play a *reves* standing firm, bending over the right knee. Then, standing firm like this, play a raking *tajo*, and another *tajo* rounded above the head in the same time, turning the whole body to the other side on the right foot, in a manner that the face ends up where you had had the back. This turn made, give the same *tajos* from before in the same order above, finishing with the last *tajo* withdrawn as said before, then the same *reves* standing firm, and a raking *tajo*, manipulating and bending the body, then a *tajo* turned above the head, armed over the right foot and giving a turn in a manner that the face ends up where you had had the back. In this way, you will understand that that which is done in the first step of this rule is done in all the rest.

Note in a Different Manner
You can do this same rule in a different manner, doing it up to the withdrawn *tajo*, and in place of a *reves*, turn on the right foot in a continuous motion with a nails-down thrust armed with the quillons high, and the point of the *montante* threatening the ground. f.124

Note
You can also do it in another manner, beginning it up to the withdrawn *tajo*, giving the *reves* and the first raking *tajo*, and then give said nails-down thrust in a continuous motion so that the face ends up where you had the back, with which you will return to do as before. Note that you can do it with 3, 4, 5, 6, *tajos*, or whichever number that you want. I speak of those that are done in the first step; the second ones that originate after the *reves*, when they are alone, have to be two, when they are with thrusts, they have to be one.

Note
This same rule can be done in turns, always making use of the withdrawn *tajo* that is said above, and in finishing one turn, another with which this is done in turns – in one turn it has to be *reveses*, then another with *tajos*, by which the last *reves* is withdrawn in the same mode of the *tajo*, but the thrust with which the *reves* turns has to be nails-up.

Declaration and Advice on the Montante
Many masters and individuals declare a rule on the *montante* wielder

withdrawing, which to me is nonsense, as they deal with it generally and without distinction. Being this way, I ask: How should one who is surrounded withdraw between his opponents? If he says withdraw after being free, that is already another time and rule. I ask how can he that guards goods and cloak withdraw, and so on? In conclusion, when one with the *montante* has to *retreat* (which is a truer name than *withdraw*), in all occasions when in an area where a *tajo* or *reves* fits, one does Rule Nine to the letter, with the steps that go forward being done backward instead. If it is a street where a *tajo* or *reves* doesn't fit,
f.125 leave with a nails-up thrust to those on the left side, and a nails-down thrust to those on the right side.

Second Declaration
If those who are surrounded have shieldmen against them, take note that all their blows will be in the low lines.

Note As for what is dealt with in Rule Two, where it says that the low blows are not necessary, it is understood that it is when they do not have any shieldmen among them, even though it may only be one.

Note The rules do not declare more than two steps (one of the left foot, and another of the right foot), because thereby all are done in a manner that, finished with the left foot, the right foot enters, and finished with the right foot, the left returns, and it continues like this until the end of the battle, alternating from one to the other.

Note When you leave from a door, if you fear enemies [are waiting] at it, put forth the point of the *montante* to one edge of the door, and then turn it to the other, going out and cutting in a continuous motion.

Rule
The *montante* positioned in its place, with the face turned to one side, commit a nails-up thrust armed over the right arm. The thrust committed, turn on the right foot, facing to the other side and lift the arms above the head, circling the *montante* in a manner that it returns to give another thrust to the same side, nails-down. Then turning the *montante* pommel to where its point goes, not giving a turn with it, but bending it over the arm, like the rule of a narrow street, give another two thrusts like those before, and more, and more to the other side. If it is necessary, one can put in a *tajo* or *reves* between two and two thrusts (that is one time) with a step of the foot in a wheel. Take

note that this rule is more florid than defensive.

PART SEVEN: SWORD AND CLOAK

First Chapter on Sword and Cloak f.126

There are those who say that the sword and cloak has particular rules. Because of that, there are many masters that demand a premium of a month (or more) to one who had never seen it, nor heard it spoken – being certain to conclude all this with simultaneously drawing the sword and readying a cloak when the opponent is close, as having to draw from afar would be called weak and timid by one who doesn't know how to do so very well. No more of this, as the real truth of the sword and cloak is just sword alone. If one responds to this that it is the same as in shield, dagger, and buckler, I say that with these three arms one can safely take a *tajo*, a *reves*, or a thrust, and not with the cloak, except in the form declared ahead.

Second Chapter: Readying the Cloak

When perhaps two opponents come together, having to draw and ready their cloaks, one will not do it simultaneously as when he draws, because being occupied in two things, he can be offended by the opponent, especially if he is quick. Rather, in drawing the sword, he moves the right shoulder so that the cloak falls from that shoulder and remains hanging on only the left shoulder. Take note that drawing the sword and the cloak falling have to be one time. Then taking back the right foot, at the same time turn back the left arm, so that the cloak remains between the arm and the body. If the opponent is distant, he can put in the foot, remaining in honest measure, putting it in with a *tajo* or nails-down or nails-up punching thrust. When he makes this diligence, he takes the arm with the cloak readied and gathered on the f.127
arm, the hand remaining inside, withdrawn in it.

When I say before "remaining in honest measure," the measure of the posture is that when the swords arrive to the thrusts, the two cannot reach much more than one palm[143] in front and no more.

Third Chapter

Entering in the fight, it is not permissible to crudely take the opponent's blows on the cloak, because although sometimes it doesn't do damage, other times it does notable damage; I have seen arms mangled from having taken blows on the cloak. It is advised that the *tajo*, when not being defended with a nails-up thrust at the eyes, is taken on the sword, where it breaks the [blow's] fury. The cloak can be given with speed in the manner of *brazal*, freeing the sword at the same time, and giving a nails-down thrust in the lower parts, or a *reves* in the legs.

Fourth Chapter

The same can be used when the opponent commits a *reves*, taking the *reves* on the sword first, and then descending a ripped *reves* or nails-down thrust to the legs. I mean to say: take it on the cloak, when not wanting to defend the *reves* with a nails-down thrust as in the rules of sword alone, which is dealt with very minutely. The counters are not pointed out here, because in the instructions of sword alone where it is dealt with separately, the counters are also dealt with.

Chapter Five: What a Counter Is

I spoke in Chapter Four that in the rules of sword alone, the counters are dealt with minutely. Many ignore them, thinking that when the
f.128 opponent executes the blow, it suffices for a counter to give another blow that does not defend from that which has been given. I say that this is obligated to cancel the thrust, *tajo*, or *reves* that is committed, and doesn't allow it to execute while giving another, which will not be called a counter, but brutality, which is the same as wild beasts and tame animals do. I say then that it would be more appropriately called a *counter* when it was only defending the opponent's blow, even though it didn't offend him, than taking one blow by giving another, since a *counter* is that which defends me from the opponent's blow, while offending him at the same time. This chapter doesn't deal with it, as these offensive and defensive counters have been touched on enough in the rules of sword alone; only the substance itself is dealt with here, in how the true counter has to be understood.

Chapter Six

In the chapters before, we deal with how one can ready the cloak and sword and be defended from the opponent, by taking the blows on the sword first. One can also ask how the thrusts offered by the opponent are defended. I say that when they are not defended with the counters of sword alone, whose rules have already been declared, they are defended when the opponent throws a nails-up thrust by gaining in the middle third of the opponent's sword and giving the response with a nails-up thrust in the chest, or slapping it with the cloak in the order and form that the *manoplados* are dealt with before.[144]

For the nails-down thrusts to the high parts, gain them with your sword to the right side in the middle third, giving a nails-down thrust in the chest, keeping in all the rest to the rule of sword alone, and when you give the thrust above nails-up, give the cloak to the opponent's sword.

PART EIGHT: SELF-DEFENSE AND TRICKS

Rules Against Treachery f.129

If two people come to insults, if one feels weak and fears that the opponent has greater advantage, or fears that he will be favored by another, he pretends that they will be brought together with good words, apologizing and saying that he doesn't want to fight with him, nor is it true what they have said, and pretends that he affirms this on the cross of his sword. In place of swearing on the cross, he quickly draws, and, as the sword leaves the scabbard, hits him in the face with the pommel. Retreating back, he makes his fight.

Second Chapter

He can do the same when they abide these reasons, saying "I swear to God[145] on this cross," and in making a cross with the fingers of the hand, pretending to kiss it, he puts the two fingers closest to the thumb in his eyes. The same has to be done in the first chapter when he goes to put the hands on the cross of the sword, he says: "I swear to God and on this cross," pretending that he swears on the cross of the sword, and it drawn as said above, making his fight as appropriate.

Third Chapter

The two being close, let the tip of your cloak be thrown over the shoulder, and when you draw, hit him in the eyes with the tip. Also, if you have it by drawing, you can do the same, but it is better being thrown.

Fourth Chapter

Being in close conversation, if one has time, put your left hand on his chest and your left foot behind his right foot, or to the side, and throw him with force. When you cannot throw the foot to him, it may be with f.130
only the hand, with all possible force.

Fifth Chapter

If you want, being close at the end of the conversation, before you draw, you can give him a slap or throw a hand to the quillons of his sword, and then draw the dagger if you carry it, which goes to the left side and not to the right, as is dealt with in its place in sword and dagger. Also, you can throw a hand to the brim of his hat and press on it to put it over his eyes. In all this, be wary that he doesn't carry a dagger with which he offends you at the same time, or when carrying it, do it cautiously as you must.

Sixth Chapter

Being in said conversations, if the opponent has his right foot out, as they are accustomed to many times, give him a kick on the outside and, if he draws, take his quillons with your hand.

Chapter Seven: the Cloak in the Horns

When (perhaps by your disgrace) you have enemies that at times are waiting for you, at night as well as during the day, make use of a trick: in the right pocket, bring a little bit of sand, the finest that you can find. When they begin drawing, take the sand and scatter it at the eyes. Take great advantage of this trick, especially at night, because if you are attacked then by one as well as by more, do the same —especially when cloak wielders want to wave their cloak and confront you — do the same, carrying a provision of sand in the pocket on the left side, and after the battle begins, go continually putting a hand in it, taking it and scattering it in their faces, and pay much attention to this in extreme.

note this rule takes advantage, taking you alone in a house

the cloak can be thrown like at a bull
the hat can be lowered over the eyes

Praise to you, Christ, eternal King
1599

PART NINE: GENERAL ADVICE

First Chapter: How Understanding the Art is Greater than Doing It

f.131

Cicero's second book *De Officiis* gives much praise to Pompey, and by extension Caesar, for the skill and knowledge with which he orders his battles. I recall that the same Cicero praises the works of understanding much more than those of the body, and says that just as the soul exceeds the body in greatness, certainly the works of understanding exceed the bodily works and exercises; the understanding of those of the body and their execution belongs to the soul.

Note how ingenuity is higher than execution of the art

In the Olympic stadium, it was the custom in some festivals to give prizes to those that ran best – seeing this blindness, the sage Diogenes started to run with a horse, and as the horse ran more, said that the prize was to be given to the horse — and implying in this advice that it was bodily work, and that it didn't have to do with understanding, so then if the prize is to be given for bodily forces and running, it has to be given to the horse for running more than the man, to be given to the lion, to the tiger, to the dragon, etc., because they have more strength than man — so it should not be given to other than the ingenuity of man who, with it, tames, subdues, and subjects ferocious animals: The speed of the horse, the strength of the bull, the ferocity of the lion, the quickness of the cheetah,[146] etc. It may be seen many times how in dangerous battles, the small force of the opponent is seen defeating the multitude of the enemy, only because of the ingenuity of able captains, as may be seen in our Spain in the time of the great soldier, the grand emperor Carlos the Great,[147] defeating the king of France[148] and capturing him and Suleiman[149] — with a much smaller force than theirs — with only his ingenuity of war.

Second Chapter: Note How the Master Doesn't Have to Play, but Teach

So the serious master, though he may be provoked to play, doesn't have to accept it after having professed and published the name of teaching, even with another master, as he doesn't profess to defend the weapons with exercise, as soldiers defend it, but to defend them like sergeant majors, teaching with the advice and stratagems that are required of them.

f.132

Third Chapter: How the Senior Masters Have to Note the People That They Examine

It has long been the case that the senior masters[150] these days set their eyes more on the person that comes to be examined than on the interest of his prize. It must be done as carefully as the relieving of his conscience matters to him, setting their eyes on the dignity of the weapons, as these days, those licensed by the king to be masters
in India
of arms, and well-regarded, set their eyes on the Nairs[151] that they have for honor and the badge of their honors, and not like today that there are those who claim master only for a thousand offenses of God and the righteous. He that would have this office must be collected, serious, exemplary, honest, zealous about weapons, peaceful, and not otherwise.

Fourth Chapter: What is Freeing the Sword

Those who think that freeing the sword is only escaping from the opponent's sword when he tests or gains it ignore much, taking the sword to the outside in a manner that it stays outside of the opponent's, without understanding that for that I only test or gain it so that he frees it, so that at the time that he goes to free it, I give him the blow that was intended — The manner that you free has to be, after the opponent has tested or gained your sword, or before he arrives to test it, to go running with your sword on the same side where you are armed until you go to leave close to the quillons of the opponent's sword, and leaving, straighten the thrust to the side that the three general rules have shown you.

Fifth Chapter: What is a Counter

One should not think that a counter is undoing the opponent's blow; when the enemy does no more than defend himself; that can be vividly called a defense that contains the other's blow. Because of that, the true counter has to be offensive in a manner that one is defended from the enemy, and at the same time offends the opponent. In this way,
f.133
it can be called a counter, as I not only undo my opponent's thought, what's more, he fell into the trap that I had armed, like another at hand.

Sixth Chapter: What is Speed and How Speed is Not Always Necessary

As for me, I think that many ignore what speed is, because blows are given with much agility, it should be called this, and not "speed." Speed is nothing more than one committing the technique[152] against your opponent in that point and condition that the enemy has given a door for it to enter, in a manner that the enemy has barely started to open it when the opponent throws himself in. The *diestro* notes that this setting off doesn't always have to be with agility, as many of us have seen in battles, as well as in individual fights, because they throw themselves in without consideration, they fall in the case of ambushes, for which occasion those on horse have the captain, and those on foot have the sergeant. This is called *agility*, so that speed is one thing, and agility is another.

PART TEN: SWORD ALONE, CONTINUED

Chapter One-Hundred Fifty-Seven: The Counters of the Elbow are in Their Place Before

Being established in whichever posture that one may be, if your opponent runs a nails-up thrust to the eyes, rip it with a *tajo* to the elbow while retreating. If the enemy continues the same thrust, rip with a *tajo* to the head, or nails-up thrust by the edges. When you rip, you can rip the *tajo* to the head, and if the enemy parries nails-up with the point high, then you can give the blow in the elbow as said above.

Chapter One-Hundred Fifty-Eight

When established nails-up, if the opponent tests your sword, it is said that you free to thrust nails-down to the chest. This thrust could be defended nails-up, gaining the opponent's sword in the cross on the outside, opening the arm the most that one will be able, and the thrust has to press to the navel.

Chapter One-Hundred Fifty-Nine

In my opinion, the thrust which is dealt with in Chapter One-Hundred Fifty-Eight can be converted to a *tajo*. When the opponent tests your sword, free by cutting with a *tajo* from the wrist with all possible speed, in a manner that he has barely tested when the *tajo* is given. So that the *tajo* leaves better when he tests you, let your sword break toward the floor.

Chapter One-Hundred Sixty: Note – This Will Be Used with Lefties f.134

When you are armed with your opponent, take note that if he plays a ripped *tajo*, you play another. If the opponent plays a *reves*, you give another *tajo* rounded above the head in a manner that the opponent has barely started the *reves* when you have given the *tajo*.

Chapter One-Hundred Sixty-One: They Do Not Bring Counters So Far

Take note that in the manner and layout that you order the *tajo*, you will order the *reves;* in this manner, you will play a *tajo* if the opponent gives another *tajo*, and respond with a *reves* if the opponent responds with a *reves*. The *reves* barely withdraws and start declining when you leave with another *reves* declined and rounded like the *tajo*, in a manner that you respond to a *tajo* with a *tajo*, and respond to a *reves* with a *reves*.

Chapter One-Hundred Sixty-Two

Being established nails-up or committing a nails-up thrust, if the opponent gains your sword, leave by the point with a *tajo* as said before. If the enemy lifts the body of the sword to undo the *tajo*, turn from the wrist below his sword to thrust nails-down to the waist, remaining protected by the quillons. You can also, in place of the thrust, leave this with a *reves* to the head and shoulder that remains uncovered. When you leave, if the opponent continues a nails-up thrust, give a *balanzada* or nails-up thrust by the same edges.

Chapter One-Hundred Sixty-Three

If the opponent throws a *tajo*, you can dodge the body and sword so that it passes in vain and commit a nails-up or nails-down thrust. If the opponent rips, before it arrives to your sword, leave with a *tajo* with the wrist, rounded with much speed. If you want, in place of a *tajo*, give a nails-down thrust, but the *tajo* is good and safe.

f.135

Chapter One-Hundred Sixty-Four

The opponent lifting with a *tajo*, quickly commit a nails-up thrust to the eyes. If the opponent descends in order to undo the thrust, it was dealt with before that one has to free and return to give the same thrust, because when the opponent starts declining to defend and impede the thrust, it has to be with speed. This speed has to carry force, and if this force doesn't find resistance in the sword, the blow will lower almost to the floor. In this time, said thrust can be given – but this thrust can be converted into a rounded *tajo* with the wrist or into an ordinary *reves*.

One-Hundred Sixty-Five

Throwing a *reves* to the legs in whatever posture that the opponent will be, besides the remedies that we dealt with before, the opponent can take the parry nails-down in a manner that your sword remains outside of the enemy's left leg, and give a nails-down thrust in the thigh.

Chapter One-Hundred Sixty-Six: Tajo, Reves – In These Two Will Not Remake Tajo, Reves

Armed nails-up, throw a *tajo*, withdrawing yourself. Against this *tajo*, the opponent throws a *reves* (take note that in the *tajo* starting, the *reves* starts). He that throws the *reves* remains uncovered on the left side. You will then be able to throw another *tajo* turned above the head, which the opponent can defend with a nails-up thrust to the eyes. If the *tajo* goes to the head, the opponent that threw the *reves* in response to the *tajo* may throw a nails-down thrust to the eyes or chest in place of the *reves*. If they rip this thrust with a *reves*, when said *reves* starts, you start off with a rounded *tajo* with the wrist, in a manner that your sword is not found by the opponent's.

Chapter One-Hundred Sixty-Seven

You can make use of the same, being armed like this, committing a withdrawn *reves*. Because this *reves* uncovers the left side, the opponent may respond with a *tajo*. He that threw the *reves* may return with another *reves* turned with the wrist, which is defended with a nails-down thrust to the eyes. If the *reves* goes to the head, in place of the *tajo* with which one responds to the *reves*, one commits a nails-up thrust. If the opponent rips the thrust, when it starts, you start off with a *reves* to the head with such speed that the opponent's sword doesn't f.136
meet yours. Be sure to note these two lessons.

Chapter One-Hundred Sixty-Eight

Being established nails-up, gain the opponent's sword to the middle. If the opponent consents, commit a nails-up thrust to the eyes, not moving yourself. If the opponent lifts, drop the same thrust to the belly, retreating back at the same time as this thrust. The opponent isn't obligated to lift, but can give a *balanzada* or free it by the same edge nails-up thrust to the eyes.

Chapter One-Hundred Sixty-Nine

Established in whatever manner that one may be, if they cross low and give the nails-up thrust, turning below the opponent's sword nails-up as it is dealt with before, and if the opponent lifts with a *tajo* to the head, give the nails-up thrust in the mode that it is given when it originates from high crossed nails-up.

Chapter One-Hundred Seventy

Established nails-up, if the opponent lowers the sword retreating the body, continue a nails-up thrust at the eyes. If the opponent gains your sword to the last thirds, when he does it, give a *tajo* in the shins (so that he ends behind him), in the manner that it is all in one time. Giving the blow, lift your sword point to the sky, because he is able to turn with a *reves*, and with it you will take the parry.

Chapter One-Hundred Seventy-One

From this same chapter above, one can make use of a nails-down thrust, *tajo* in the face, *reves* in the back, keeping to the rule of the
f.137 same *tajo* above, in that mode of attacking. The *tajo* that goes to the face frees by the point of the opponent's sword. The thrust has to be in the belly, and the *reves* in the back, keeping in all the parry in said chapter.

Chapter One-Hundred Seventy-Two[153]

Established nails-up or in whatever manner that you will be, threaten a nails-up thrust at the eyes. If he lifts, give the same nails-up thrust in the breast of the right side, withdrawing back with the ordinary step. The opponent continuing, return with the techniques[154] that serve in such place.

Chapter One-Hundred Seventy-Three

Before, we dealt with a nails-down thrust that originates after the two are crossed nails-down, and is given nails-down to the chest, the swords remaining together, as follows: the opponent's as it was, and yours close to the quillons in a manner that your head remains covered. I say now that if the opponent lowers when you give said nails-down thrust, turn a *tajo* to the face with the wrist, or the same thrust to the eyes.

GODINHO'S NOTES [155]

Palms f.2

The two shieldmen established, one of them sways the body back and the sword toward the floor. If the opponent commits a nails-up thrust, rip with a *tajo* – Take note that the opponent has to take the blow on the shield and put himself in, giving a nails-down thrust in the thigh or belly. This counter being noticed at the time that you rip, retreat the foot back, so that the *tajo* that goes to the head instead cuts in between the sword and shield, which is ripping from chest to chest, because if you do not withdraw, ripping with a *tajo* is false, and like this it is safe.

that nails-up thrust when he lifts with a *tajo* that is withdrawn from me
in the shield, paper remains for 8 rules
more paper remains for an attack against many
and remains for advice
remember to be able to give falls and kicks in the belly
in the advice of shield a page remains
these things are declared because when the lessons come, there is no need to touch them
how the parry of the *tajo* and *reves* will be made
the step with a blow
given that a lesson is in different manners many times
how there is only one *tajo*, one *reves*, and one nails-down or nails-up thrust
how they're not called quillons
the gainings
the sword has two weapons
that a technique[156] is not committed twice
remember freeing

Firstly f.3

the obligation of the senior master ____________________ c 3 f 12[157]
of the other masters ________________________________ f 18 c 8
of the disciple ____________________________________ f 19
how the sword has to be taken from the floor __________ f 16
how the sword has to be gripped ____________________ c 15
how one will draw from close ______________________ f 13

how the double arms are distinct ______________________ 67
how the shield has to move __________________________ f 75
how the arm will be in the low nails-down thrusts # against many ___
____ f 79
how the masters can make more lessons from each rule __ f 79
how all the opponent's blows can be countered with thrust, *tajo*, and
reves ____ f 80
declaration about the buckler ________________________ f 81
how the small buckler is not a weapon ________________ f 81
sword and dagger _________________________________ f 94
how the parries will be taken ________________________ f 99
how the cloak will be taken with the dagger ___________ f 108
on sword and cloak ________________________________ f 126
on the *montante* __________________________________ f 110
declaration on the *montante* ________________________ f 124 125
on the two swords _________________________________ f 83
rules against treachery _____________________________ f 129

Reminders and Order f.5

1 #[162] the obligation of the senior master
2 # the obligation of the other masters
3 # the obligation of the disciple
4 # why the bouts will be arranged
the abbreviations that go in the book
8 # how the sword has to end after playing *tajo* and *reves*
9 # what is *tajo*, *reves*, nails-up and nails-down thrust, *manoplado*, *garatusa*, *mandoble*, *manoplado*, etc.
10 # what is testing, gaining, and the danger of gaining
10 # what is freeing, and how
11 # what is a counter
12 # how the blows have to be offensive and defensive
15 # how the dagger has different techniques[163] playing against dagger or shield
13 # what is speed, and how it has to be understood
2 # how the masters do not have to be thrown into battle with similar persons, or even with any
2 # how understanding the art is a liberal art, and playing it is a mechanical art
5 # how one has to draw
6 # how the steps will be made

how one has to cut against one and more
7 # how one has to rip, and what it is
2 # how the sword will be taken from the floor
2 # how one has to settle and take the sharp sword[164] first
14 # how the double arms are distinct, but the play is all the same, and on the shield
16 # how putting in the left foot is good, understanding how
2 # how the feet have to be planted
3 # how there is no proper place or posture in the weapons
16 # how the small buckler is not safe
how the mill has wheels[165]
2 # how the steps are different against one and against many
2 # how the disciples have to begin
2 # how the blows have to be made known for vital reasons
16 # how putting in the foot is one thing and taking it back is another, I say that taking the foot back is one thing and withdrawing it is another
a withdrawn ripped *tajo* is one thing, *tajo* with the wrist is another, *tajo* with a slap is another (the mill has two wheels)
in Chapter 8 # that the players surround water
for what reason they enter with left or right foot
how whoever says that one who is gained has no remedy is wrong how he that is gained has to make use of the counters of the thrust that is turned nails-down
that in a battle, one cannot keep step with perfection, which costs much feeling in the lance, horse, shield, rein, opponent, and land
that the opinion of gaining the weak of the opponent's sword with the strong is false, as that strength is based on the resistance that the opponent makes, then if he doesn't make it, it serves no more than to be in danger if the opponent frees
how the sword has to be gripped and where the thumb has to be placed naturally
how the more they gain the sword, the more danger they are in,
f.6 because the more the king is put into the opponent's land, the closer the opponent is to him, and the more his life is in danger
that the step has to originate with the foot that is lifted, and not in that which stays, and thus when they retreat back, the body and all goes
that one that commits the technique[166] of thrust, *tajo*, or *reves* goes forewarned, like the good captain is supplied before giving battle, and the good thief
how speed is attached to understanding, and understanding works

first
by the signs and reasons, a man knows that which is hidden – I say that when you have to commit some technique, that you will not reveal by similar things before you act
that one should not understand measuring for the reason that passion has no place, and when one has to be with that, he can measure inside after gaining – only that in place of step is good judgment, sense, and understanding of the impassioned served, that even in those things, passion blinds and makes that that which is deserved by one is given to another who doesn't deserve it
one can know by touch when the opponent lifts, but note that he lifts before going, as follows: when the tree is not made to see the air with great heat, by the flight of the branches one comes to understand that it does it, but when the river runs, if you go to show that which goes in it, when you reach with the finger, it already goes running and is the same water
that skill and knowing are not the same
if the thrusts on the inside have to be nails-down or nails-up
if the nails-down posture is valued as much as that of nails-up

§1 f.7

On page 37, the danger that there is in testing[167] a sword is dealt with. When one has to test, it has to be on the point, swaying the body toward the rear, because the same word[168] denotes caution of the opposing side, as well as the same manner that the soldier goes fearfully when plunging into the enemy's ground by order of his captain. As soon as he doesn't recognize the place where he is and the danger that he is in, he goes with caution and feeling[169]; this is feeling around[170] and recognizing. It has to be done so when one wants to test the opponent's sword; it has to appear to the opponent to not be falsified, as declared in its chapters, and there are different blows between testing and gaining. He that passes the ford goes feeling[171] fear.

§2

Speed has to be understood, whenever it touches on the parry of single and double arms, that he commits the blow with too much speed, without considering the danger of the opponent, what happens to him is that which happens to the knight that, seeing a Moor, attacked him with much speed, without considering the danger, and found himself deceived with an ambush. For attacking, speed doesn't have a proper place, and it is the same in the counters.

§3
The obligations of the senior master close to the persons that he examines, as he has to be informed of their lives, on the occasion that he is seen to proceed with them, especially that he doesn't have to examine solitary men. Men that finish, leaving from their master, can request a letter of examination without more exercise, not putting their eyes on the interest.
§4
It is no little obligation to know how the sword has to end when a *tajo* or *reves* is played, because if perhaps it will be necessary to rip, it is very important for the sword to end in its place, in a manner that when throwing a *tajo*, the sword ends nails-up, and giving a *reves*, the sword ends nails-down.
§5
There are many opinions that the left foot does not have to be put in for the committed blows of thrust, *tajo*, or *reves*. Separating myself from this opinion, I say that one can put in the left foot in the techniques[172] of sword alone, and double arms, as it goes declared in its place.
§6
The feet have to be planted according to the circumstances of the incident, because they don't have only one obligation in the way that they have to be planted, because firm to firm will be in one manner, retreating in another, against many in another, as declared in their places, not leaving from the natural walk.
§7
I see different questions asked on which is the best posture and how one goes, as if in the postures (or to say better, in the weapons) it had a proper place, without noting that the good posture is that which defends me from the opponent's blow.
§8
For vital reasons, the blows that the master will teach have to be disclosed to the disciples, because in order to teach, it's not important that the master may be, it is necessary...

[missing page][173]

f.9

the more ground gained, the more danger

...the opponent's sword, because if the strong rests on mine, that the cause that I considered that if it could be, but the strength of my sword consists of the opponent's sword resisting me, that if he doesn't resist me with the weak of his sword, and frees it, deviating the body, at the press of the opponent's, it is clear that it will remain in the air in vain, so then this practice has to be treated with distinction, that even if the opponent makes resistance, the opponent can deceive, making that he resists it, like two that are pulling a rope and one releases it.

§14

By the same case I prove that, since the opponent consents to the gaining, if he consents to it knowing the techniques that originate from it, it is better than those who make it. On the other hand, he that makes the gaining takes note that he has to be very practiced and skilled in the techniques that originate from said gaining, that in another manner has the same danger as the soldier that gains ground and doesn't secure the return if it will be necessary.

§15

Those that presume they will be *diestros* support greatly that the sword has to be gripped with the thumb on the third.[174] I say that if, when the disciple had never taken the sword in hand, that it was created in that nature, but having already made a habit, in whatever other habit. I mean to say that the disciple does not have to be taken from the nature in which he is created, because natural ingenuity works much more than strength, where it is seen that in the pitched battles, the few defeat the many by having more natural ingenuity and accord – as such, if the left arm has more strength than the right, yet the right does it with more ease by being made to handle the sword, look that the left arm does the same, having more ingenuity than the right, because the left is made with habit, then the habit and custom is the cause of agile strength, that the strength alone has no place. The lion and the bull have much strength, that is to say much more than man, but the natural cleverness and accord of man defeats and tames them. As follows, the strength that they praise is not true in the fight if it is not attached to the art more than strength.

§16

Before he commits the assault, it suits the good captain to review his understanding of all the dangers ahead that the opponent can offer, in order to be defended with ease. Like the proverb says, the enemy noticed is half combated. Thus, whichever blow that you will commit to the opponent, you have to bring the counter already wrought in the understanding, and that other undone, which in another manner of attacking is a tricky thing.

f.10

§17

There should be much notice between the player and his opponent, that they don't make manipulations, nor other signs, whereby the blow that he wants to commit can be known, but rather forged in the mind, begin with the step which must execute it. Because like this, as by the movement of the tree, however little that it is, one is made to see on a hot day that there is air, without seeing it. As follows, when you test or gain the opponent's sword, see that he will know by feel when you lift. Because of that, if possible, start off with the step first, then the sword.

§18

That which is discussed as the measurement in the weapons doesn't appear as true discussion to me, because the inside play doesn't fit measurement in the gaining, nor in thought. So if one speaks to me of established play, I question if it means to be armed against the opponent in such posture that one can reach by only manipulating the body, and with only removing it he remains free. With none of these two things is there entering or leaving with the foot; it is folly, that the two will be like a bell that, without moving from one place, responds back and forth.

Mainly who had ever seen such judgment and feeling that a locked fight had measured, whether it be he that is lost caused by fear, or the impassioned with the desire of offending, or with the passion, it costs much to have feeling in the horse, in the reins, in the lance and the shield. I will call that measuring when he begins the thrust, *tajo*, or *reves* in such a manner, if it has to be committed that he may be reached with only moving the body, not putting in the foot, or with only the arm, not moving the body. In order to reach, if it is necessary to take a step, then if not put more, as many as enough that the sword reaches, the arm always remaining straight, having place, and the body outside.

§19

Some think that parrying the opponent's blow is the true counter. That can be called a parry, but a counter is undoing the opponent's intention. The intention is that I fall in the trap, as with such manner I have to defend myself from it so that he falls in it, as when the enemy is surrounding the city, that makes to enter a mine, making inside another that undoes their intentions.

Table of This Book f.11

§ One time, one who said to be a *diestro* asked me that if one is attacked by three, which should be responded to first. I told him that the one that was pressing me most – and if none, the one that was to the right side was to follow, in a manner that he on the right side always remained to the inside.

APPENDIX A: PACHECO'S THIRTY "VULGAR *TRETAS*"

Many works on *la verdadera destreza* include descriptions of the techniques of the old style (which was referred to as "common," "vulgar," or "false"); these techniques were often described as having poor execution or inappropriate timing in an attempt to denigrate and censure it. The most prolific author was Luis Pacheco de Narváez, whose works include various mentions of vulgar or common techniques, culminating in a list of the thirty *tretas*[175] of the vulgar *destreza.*

Pacheco's list of thirty *tretas* does not include only Spanish techniques, but also those of other nations; to Pacheco, any style that wasn't *la verdadera destreza* was vulgar, regardless of national origin. Alongside the old Spanish authors, he cites various Italians and a German as well, including Marozzo, Agrippa, Fabris, Giganti, di Grassi, Meyer, and others. What follows is Pacheco's list from his last work, *New Science* (*Nueva Ciencia)*, published in 1672, in contrast to Godinho's descriptions and advice of the same techniques. The text in quotes has been translated from New Science in such a way that no knowledge of the technical vocabulary is necessary.

First Treta – *Estocada de Puño* (Punching Thrust)
This is a thrust delivered in a punching motion by extending the arm forcefully. Pacheco describes it this way: "this consists of two movements, the first backward and the second forward, which is sometimes mixed with upward movement when they direct the blow to the face, and others with downward in order to wound from the chest down." He also asserts that it is done with all thrusts in the ordinary *destreza.*

Godinho equates *de puño* with the term *de aremeso,*[176] which means that it is done with the arm in the manner of throwing an object or weapon, such as a javelin. He only mentions it once in the sword alone and once with cloak, although it's more common with two swords, done immediately after a *reves* or before a *tajo.*

Second Treta – *Cornada* (Gore)
This is an ascending thrust, which is not found in Godinho's work.

Third Treta – *Botonazo* (Button Strike)
Described as gaining with a step forward with the right foot, then extending the arm in a thrust to the face.

Many times, Godinho describes gaining followed by a thrust, but the specific footwork and the name that he ascribes to the *treta* are not used by Godinho.

Fourth Treta – *Zambullida* (Dive)
Pacheco describes this as beating the opponent's sword to the outside, inclining forward, and running past the opponent with a thrust, or in more detail: "to take the opponent's sword on the outside (with a step of the right foot straight forward, or very close to it) moving it to the right side with his sword and leaving it there, free and in potency for all that he will want to do, returning the way that it went, and giving another step with the same foot (although some wanted to correct it, putting in the left foot) to wound with a thrust below in the chest, higher or lower, according to how he leaves from the folly of the force that is conveyed, and perhaps he reaches to wound in the face, and others on the floor, and even hitting the head on it: The movements of which it consists are eleven; the first two (if it begins from the sword high) are mixed downward and backward, with which the sword is lowered, the third offline to his left side, with which it is placed below and across the enemy's sword, the fourth, and fifth mixed upward and to the center; the sixth offline, with which both swords are parted to the right side, the seventh to the center, the eighth and ninth mixed downward and backward like the first, the tenth and eleventh, for the execution, forward and upward if it is to the chest or face, or forward and downward if it is low, as from there they rarely make use of the straight line."

The name given to this by Godinho is the *balanzada* thrust.[177] However, he specifically advises that it should never be done offensively (the way that Pacheco describes), but only defensively. He frequently describes it from a position of having the weight over the left leg, leaning back, which is similar to Pacheco's fourteenth *treta*, *quiebro*.

Fifth Treta – *Manotada* (Slap)
This is "making a deflection with the left hand at the point of the opponent's sword, when his sword is extended forward, or when he goes to wound with a thrust, and this with the intent of throwing his own punching thrust." Pacheco goes on two describe two methods of performing it, saying it "is able to be done from the inside to the outside (which by being done above the sword, the more learned of fencing call *rodeo*), and from the outside to the inside, which they call *bofeton*, which end in diverse lines and form opposing semicircles."

Godinho uses the term *manoplado* for the defense with the left hand against a thrust.[178] It is done to either side, or downward, but it is never done offensively, only against a thrust.

Sixth Treta – *Estocada a la Mano* (Thrust to the Hand)
Pacheco describes this as a form of punching thrust, "and thus it consists of two movements, backward and forward, and if the sword is low one more is necessary, which has to be upward mixed with the forward: Among the authors, only Pedro de la Torre makes mention of it, and with particular appreciation, orders that it is thrown to the right hand, affirming that to whomever it will be executed will lose sense."

Godinho thrusts to the hand as a counter to a *tajo* or *reves*. He also describes doing it to an established opponent, but makes no mention of withdrawing the hand first or any connection to the punching thrust.

Seventh Treta – *Encadenada* (Enchained)
This appears in two places in *New Science* – as the seventh vulgar *treta* with sword alone, and also as the first vulgar *treta* with sword and dagger. The latter is described by Pacheco in this way: "they throw a thrust below and to the outside of the sword, directed to the right side, which for our knowledge (although sinning against propriety) we call a 'thrust of the whole circle,' and at the same time they put the dagger between their right arm and the point of the opposing sword, and deflecting it to the inside above their own sword, applying new force with the downward movement, they press and subject it." Done with the sword alone (which Pacheco says is a modern invention), the upper quillon (on the thumb side of the hilt) is used in place of the dagger.

Only the sword-and-dagger version is done by Godinho, and he advises it quite frequently, including various ways to set it up or counter it.[179]

Eighth Treta – *Enarcada* (Arched)
This is a very old *treta*, according to Pacheco, which consists of turning the hand to nails-down and curving the arm to thrust around the opponent's sword on the inside. He describes two variations: "the first is done preceding on the part of its creator a gaining on the opponent's sword, and if this is consented to, a thrust is made to the face; and if this is deflected, he turns the hand so that the weak of the opposing sword falls on the strong of his, curving the arm, sometimes putting in the right foot, and other times the left, executing the blow in the face or chest. The other mode is if the opponent makes the gaining, to turn the hand, curve the arm, and wound where it has been said. The first consists of seven movements: upward, offline, downward, to the center and forward mixed, with which the gaining is finished, and the last two for the attack: backward for the bend of the arm, and forward in order to wound. In the second form there are three movements: upward, with which that part of subjection that the gaining does is resisted, backward in

order to turn the arm and hand nails-down, and forward for the blow."

Godinho does not give this movement a name, and only refers to it as turning the hand nails-down. He uses it frequently as a counter to a nails-up thrust by the same edges, usually inclining the head and shoulders to the left side. It is mentioned as a counter to gaining, but done by stepping in and capturing the opponent's quillons with the left hand. The same technique is used by Luis Díaz de Viedma, an author of *la verdadera destreza* who was formerly a vulgar fencer.

Ninth Treta – *Engavilanada* (Crossguarded)

This *treta* involves using the cross of the sword (which is often quite long), to beat the opponent's sword point to the side, followed by a thrust. It is not found in Godinho's work.

Tenth Treta – *Torneada* (Turned)

Pacheco says that this is half-bred between Flemish and Spanish; it involves gaining on the inside and continuing to turn around to deliver a two-handed thrust.[180] It is not found in Godinho's work.

Eleventh and Twelfth Treta – *Remeson* (Diminishing) and *Golpe a la Espada* (Blow to the Sword)

The *golpe a la espada* is described by Pacheco as a *tajo* or *reves* to the opponent's sword, with the intent to knock it from his hand. The *remeson* is a more modern version, where the blow is directed down the opponent's blade, sliding from the tip to the hilt, pushing the sword to the side. Neither technique is described by Godinho, although he does describe how to counter an opponent attempting to beat your sword away.

Thirteenth Treta – *Llamar* (Inviting)

Pacheco writes that "its formation is in two modes – the one, throwing a small half horizontal *tajo* with moderate force, carrying his sword to the left side a little more or less low, making a forward extreme with the body and uncovering the chest; the other is done with a half *reves* to carry the sword to the right side, curving the arm and uncovering the breadth. The intent that they bring in this, and the apparent imagination with which they are tricked and satisfied, is (said in their language) to stimulate or to invite the opponent that they go to wound them in the opening, to meet the sword (we repeat their term) and enter the left foot to execute their celebrated *zambullida* in the chest or face, or some of the others." He further states that "Jayme Pons was the first (among those that up to now have been seen) that ordered that the opponent was deceived with the posture, uncovering some part of the body where he is inspired to wound; Francisco Román dealt with inciting or inviting the opponent with the same intent."

Although he does not use the same terminology, Godinho does advise throwing false or lost *tajos* in order to counter the opponent's attack into the opening. He also frequently describes positions in which the sword is held leaving you open for a thrust, giving the counters to these thrusts. Additionally, when Godinho describes what a *treta* ("trick") is, he mentions presenting an opening to the opponent.[181]

Fourteenth Treta – *Quiebro* (Bend)
This is a posture in which "after established, the *diestro* drops back, making a large extreme over the left foot, putting the sword in the low line." He also mentions that foreigners make use of it, and of the authors, "the first which one was able to find was Jayme Pons, from whose works the honorific praise was drawn, judging the unworthiness of its qualification, who said that the sword has to sometimes be placed across the legs, and the quillons close to the right hip."

Godinho describes this posture several times, along with using the *balanzada* thrust to counter the committed attacks from the opponent that it exposes you to.

Fifteenth Treta – *Final*
This is a count-clockwise circling action around the opponent's blade, ending with a thrust on the inside, beneath the opponent's sword. This is not found in Godinho's work.

Sixteenth Treta – *Garatusa*
This is a circling blade action, done either counter-clockwise or clockwise that envelops and moves the opponent's blade. Pacheco says that although its invention is claimed by many, it originated in "our regions." He describes it as being done "on the inside and on the outside, and these two differences are directed to the same end; the mode how the first is formed is to place his sword above the opposing, for deviating it toward his right side, and left of the opponent, giving a step with the right foot, they put their body in that unoccupied place in order to wound with a thrust in the chest on the outside, with the opposing sword free for whatever he will want to do. All this consists of seven movements (if the combatants each have the swords extended forward): the first is upward in order to raise the sword, the second offline to his left side, the third and fourth mixed downward and offline to the right line with which the opposing sword and his move aside, the fifth to the center, leaving the adversary's sword where the third and fourth finished, the sixth upward, and the last forward, for the thrust."

For the second version, "there are ten movements, and a circle is made as large as the interval of the arm and sword; the first movement is natural, the second offline to the left side with which it is placed below and across the opposing sword, the third and fourth mixed upward and to the center, until being joined to it, the fifth offline to the right side, with which the deflection is done, the sixth and seventh natural and offline, with which they propel it to the left side, and the circle is finished closing, which is done with the whole arm, the eighth and ninth to the center and upward, in order to place the sword in the way, and the last forward in order to execute the thrust, leaving the opponent's sword free in those last three."

Godinho describes only the first (counter-clockwise) variation, and does not include the thrust as a part of the *garatusa*.

Seventeenth Treta – *Ganancia* (Gaining)
Placing the sword above and across the opponent's sword, which "has to consist of three movements: upward, offline, and downward." Pacheco also writes about doing the same without making any contact between the swords, which he calls gaining in the air.

Godinho advises gaining frequently, and defines it as taking control of the middle of the opponent's sword with the middle (or sometimes the strong) of you own.

Eighteenth Treta – *Tentada* (Tested)
Pacheco says that this "was only native among our compatriots, and as venerated by them as it was little received in other provinces." He describes it as beginning with the previous *treta* – "they make a gaining, placing their sword over the opposing one, with a little reinforcement on it, presuming that the resistant force that is opposed to this will cause some upward movement, in order to be able to enter below (leaving it free) and wound with a thrust in the belly."

This is used extensively by Godinho, who defines it as the point of the sword reaching to the point of the opponent's sword. He advises various subsequent techniques, depending upon the opponent's reaction, rather than presuming that it will be resisted.

Nineteenth Treta – *Arrebatar y Tajo* (Beat Away and Cut)
As described in *New Science*, "they give a blow to it with theirs from below on the inside with the intent of deflecting it from that position, and they form a *tajo,* giving a step with the right foot to its
side, which they call a change of feet, although they usually abbreviate this transit, and give it straight forward. The movements of which it consists are four, two downward, one offline, and one upward; the first, to be made unequal to the

common place in which they are established; the second, offline, to be placed below and across the opposing sword, the upward to give the blow and make the deflection, and the last is the downward with which they execute the *tajo*."

This description is very similar to what Godinho calls a *ripping tajo* (*romper de tajo*), although the ripping tajo is only done defensively. Godinho does mention how to counter the opponent attempting the beat your sword away (*arebater*), but does not describe the manner in which it's done.

Twentieth Treta – *Codazo* (Cut to the Elbow)
Wounding the right arm of the opponent, this "consists of gaining, an attack, a half horizontal *reves*, two steps, and nine movements: the three for the gaining and the step with the right foot (that such times we have said), to the center and forward to attack without departing from the sword (as if it will be parted, the upward movement will be necessary) already are known, and the offline to the left side mixed with the downward to be placed below the opponent's sword, also known, then the half *reves* [composed of two movements] given in the elbow (by which it took the denomination of *codazo*) with which they make the retreat."

Godinho often describes a *tajo* or *reves* to the arm, usually in counter to a cut or a thrust. Only once does he refer to it as a *codazo*.[182]

Twenty-First Treta – *Brazal* (Bracer)
This *treta* is the name given to parrying and detaining the opposing sword with the arm. Those who perform this technique often wore a steel armband or even a plank of wood on their forearm under their sleeve. Done in many different ways, Pacheco describes it this way in *New Science*: "When the opponent's sword is forward (and nowhere else, as its potency does not extend to more) they place theirs below, and without deflecting it to one side or the other, they raise it up, as much as the stature of he who does it, and then they apply the left arm that detains it in order to be able to wound with a thrust, giving two steps: the first with the right foot and the other with the left."

Godinho says that *brazal* is not safe and has no place in sword alone. With the cloak, he advises using the cloak in the manner of *brazal* after having parried with the sword.

Twenty-Second Treta – *Canillazo* (Cut to the Shin)
Pacheco writes that it is done in three ways: "The first starts by the gaining and attack, and if the opponent lifts the sword due to fear, they pass the body giving a step, sometimes with the right foot, and others with the left, executing the *tajo* in

the right leg... The second mode is by means of the *arrebatar* on the inside, and for that the most times they make use of the inviting... the last mode, which is *arrebatar* on the outside for a *reves*, it is only by this measure, or accumulating it from the inviting." He also says that Jaime Pons advised that all cuts are thrown to the legs when armed with a buckler, that "it has been with equal fortune accepted by all, and although Jayme Pons was not who invented it (because only ignorance can be its progenitor) he had guilt in placing it by one of its expensive preventions."

In the first form described, Godinho advises giving a *tajo* to the shins after a thrust is gained on the inside, but isn't clear about stepping in or not. The second is similar to what is described with the shield as a ripped *tajo* to the legs, and the third form is similar to a ripped *reves* to the legs to counter a thrust. He also generally advises a cut to the legs while retreating, but in the section against lefties, advises attacking directly with a *tajo* the legs. He says that with double arms, the low cuts are better, and explicitly mentions some to the shins.

Twenty-Third Treta – *Treta Doble* (Double Technique)
This *treta* is composed of two cuts in succession. Various sources ascribe particular cuts and targets to it; Pacheco in *New Science* defines it as a *tajo* to the legs followed by another to the head.

Twenty-Fourth and Twenty-Fifth *Tretas* – *Tajo y Reves Horizontal* (Horizontal *Tajo* and *Reves*)
Rather than any horizontal cut, these refer to cuts which are given at waist level, with an extreme forward bend of the body. The theory of *la verdadera destreza* describes various lines along the body used for reference points; "there is one that is called 'horizontal,' and this divides him by his length in equal parts, and comes across the belt, from which they took the name of this *tajo* and *reves*, because they pass horizontally (although some called them broken, or ripped, and others long *reves* and *tajo)*."

With the shield, Godinho gives a *tajo* to the waist once, without advising any sort of forward lean, and does not call it horizontal.[183]

Twenty-Sixth and Twenty-Seventh *Tretas* – *Tajo y Reves Ascendiente* (Ascending *Tajo* and *Reves)*
These are rising cuts, of which Pacheco says that the Italians are fond. Godinho only describes a *tajo* that cuts from knee to head twice.[184]

Twenty-Eighth Treta – *Escampavita* (Escaping)
Pacheco states that this is native to Italy and presumes that Camillo Agrippa is its

progenitor. He wrote that it is done in two ways: "the first, in which Agrippa left it placed, is to establish the right arm and enter, searching for that which they call *measure*, which comes to be something closer than the mean of proportion, and without arriving to the opposing sword, and being in distance of being able to reach him with an extreme turn of the body, they turn the left leg, having it cross the right as much as than they can to the rear, such that the point of the foot (leaving the heel lifted) comes to the same distance as the right, turning the face to the left side, and lowering the head in order to protect it with the quillons (with which they don't see where they wound, nor where they can be wounded), they execute a thrust in the chest. With the second, he had to presume to amend some presumed genius, to which he would make advised the risk and misfortunes of the first, in leaving the opposing sword free from beginning to end, and wanted that it was started by the gaining on it."

This same footwork is described by Godinho, who calls it a "wheeling step" (*pie de rueda*).

Twenty-Ninth Treta – *Irremediable* (Unstoppable)
This is described by Pacheco as gaining the opponent's blade while stepping forward with the right foot, then stepping forward with the left, putting the left shoulder forward, and wounding with a thrust. This is not found in Godinho's work.

Thirtieth Treta – *Defendida* (Defended)
A thrusting feint to the face, followed by the arm and sword being withdrawn, then entering and thrusting again. This is not found in Godinho's work.

APPENDIX B: GLOSSARY

Arrebatar ("to beat away")
Removing something with violence and force.

Balanzada
Although this can be directly translated as "balanced," it does not imply a state of resting equilibrium as it does in English. Rather, it refers to the motion of a balance or scale used to determine weight: a back-and-forth movement. It's applied to a body shifting its weight forward and backward, and is also used to refer the rocking motion of a ship at sea. It can mean swaying, waving, tilting, swinging, or rocking.

Brazal
This is the name for a piece of armor that covers the arm. It was also used as the name for a technique that involves using the left arm to detain the opponent's sword, or even using it to parry a cut. Those who utilize this technique often wore a piece of armor over their forearm, under their sleeve.

De Puño
The word *puño* means both hilt and fist; a thrust done *de puño* means to deliver it in a punching motion by extending the arm forcefully. Godinho equates it with the term *de aremeso*, which means that it is done with the arm in the manner of throwing an object or weapon, such as a javelin.

Destreza ("skill")
The literal meaning is "skill" or "dexterity," though it later came to also mean skill with a sword –fencing.

Diestro
One who is skilled at something. This term was used to mean someone who was practiced at swordsmanship, but not yet a master (*maestro*).

Encadenado ("enchained")
Enchained or shackled – having been rendered unable to move or take action.

Espada Blanca ("sharp sword")
Literally "white sword," they were often highly polished, leading to the name.

Espada Negra / Preta ("practice sword")
Literally "black sword," practice swords had no edge and a button tip, and were often unpolished.

Firmado ("established")
Steadied, made firm or secure. In swordplay, used to mean that one stands on guard, often holding the point of the sword at the opponent. Also *afirmado.*

Ganar ("to gain")
This word generally means to obtain something sought after or contested by someone else. It is also used in a military context to refer to conquering territory.

Garatusa
Possibly meaning scribble or scrawl (poorly-formed writing), this refers to a technique done by circling the sword around the opponent's, keeping contact between the blades in order to move the opponent's sword out of position.

Librar ("to free")
To free or escape, to liberate or remove from another's control.

Maestro ("master")
Fencing masters were examined and certified in particular weapons or weapon combinations. Since at least the 14th century, there have been royal fencing masters which served the crown.

Maestro Mayor ("senior master")
This office was established in the 15th century as the chief master and examiner of a kingdom or vice-royalty.

Mandoble
A blow given by using the wrist. Although today it refers to something two-handed (from *mano doble* – double hand), during the time of Godinho it referred to a bending (*doblar*) the wrist to strike a blow; Minsheu (1599) defined it as "a blow stricken by doubling the hand backward."

Manoplado
Presumably from the word *manopla,* the name of a piece of armor which protects the hand, known in English as a gauntlet. Godinho uses this term to name a technique that involves deflecting a thrust with the left hand.

Mesura ("salute")
An outward show of respect and courtesy. It also means moderation, restraint, composure, or measure.

Palmo ("palm")

One palm is a unit of length corresponding to roughly 20 cm or 8 in.

Pie de Rueda ("wheeling step")
A step given with the left foot by pivoting backwards around the right foot until the back is almost turned to the opponent.

Rasgar / Romper ("to rip")
Literally meaning to rip or break, *romper* also means to break the continuity of something fluid. Militarily, it also means to disrupt a formation of armed men.

Regla ("rule")
Rule, order, statue, precept, principle, or method of doing something. Godinho teaches two swords and *montante* through rules, and often uses the term interchangeably with "chapter."

Revés
Simply meaning reverse, opposite, or contrary, this refers to a backhand cut – from the point of view of a right-handed swordsman, it cuts from left to right.

Tajo
Literally meaning simply a cut or a slice, this refers to a forehand cut – from the point of view of a right-handed swordsman, it cuts from right to left.

Tentar ("to test")
Testing, feeling, tempting, probing, trying, instigating, feel around or examine something with the sense of touch, especially without being able to see. *Tentar* comes from the same Latin root as the English word tentative.

Tiempo
Although the literal translation is "time," this word is frequently used by Godinho in places where in modern English we would say "technique."

Treta ("trick")
This refers to a trick or a deceit used in fencing, such as a feint or false attack to evoke a defense which is evaded with a different attack, or presenting a false opening to provoke an attack by the opponent. The authors of *la verdadera destreza* used the term differently, however; to them, *treta* is a plan of action, or a technique which is formed in the mind and executed with an intended outcome.

ENDNOTES

1. Viterbo, S., A esgrima em Portugal. p.10
2. Bells hom Affrahim, Jewish Mallorcan, fencing master of Juan I of Aragón in 1389. Llabrés, G.., "Un maestro de esgrima de Juan I" BSAL (1890); III(128): 321.
3. Copin Gallant, fencing master to the king of Navarre in 1414. Yanguas y Miranda, J., Diccionario de antiguedades del Reino de Navarra. t.I, p.395
4. Ceballos-Escalera Gila, A. Sanchez de Lollano Prieto, J., "El Maestro mayor de la destreza de las armas" Colaboraciones (1997) 6: 77-108
5. This, in and of itself, is somewhat unique to other countries, where the role of the fencing master was relegated to wealthy trade guilds, such as in the German-speaking territories, or the lower classes, such as in England and France, but were wholly outside any formal connection to the nobility. See, for example, Anglo, Sydney, The Martial Arts of Renaisssance Europe, Yale University Press (2000).
6. Examen en Palma de Mallorca en el patio del castillo de la Almudaina. Llompart, G., "Ideal caballeresco y escuela de esgrima en Mallorca en el siglo XV," CHJZ (1976-7) 29-30: 149-161
7. Valle, M., Nueva Bibliografia. (.374)
8. Examen de Arnaut de Castellbò en Palma de Mallorca. Llompart, G., "Ideal caballeresco y escuela de esgrima en Mallorca en el siglo XV," CHJZ (1976-7) 29-30: 149-161
9. Because the Iberian two-handed sword has a very particular size and form, I refer to it throughout the text by its Iberian name.
10. Pons is principally known through the work of a 17th-century master, Luis Pacheco de Narvaez, who quotes from him quite extensively in his Nueva Ciencia (1632). A compilation and translation of these quotes may be found at Rivera, Tim. References to the fencing treatise of Jaime Pons de Perpiñan http://www.spanishsword.org/files/references.pons.pdf (accessed 8/28/2014)
11. Valle, M., Nueva Bibliografia (.446)
12. Pacheco's Nueva Ciencia is again our principle source for our knowledge of de la Torre's method, but he is also cited by the 17th-century Italian master, Giuseppe Pallavicini in his La Scherma Illustrata (1670). A compilation and translation of these quotes may be found in Rivera, Tim. References to the fencing treatise of Pedro de la Torre. http://www.spanishsword.org/files/references.delatorre.pdf (accessed 8/28/2014)
13. Valle, M., Nueva bibliografía (.400)
14. In Italy we see a movement from focus on the two-handed sword, to the sword and

buckler to the sword alone, possibly reflective of the move from knightly battle-field combat to civilian self-defense and dueling. In Iberia the situation is less clear. Pons seems to have put sword and buckler as primary, and de la Torre (same year) seems to have sword alone as primary. Roman is difficult to pin down, but definitely isn't a move away from two-handed sword as primary (he is actually credited with fleshing it out more).

15. Román is quoted extensively by Pacheco, but also by Carranza, the founder the "new school" of fencing that was opposed to the methods of masters such as Pons, de la Torre and Román.). A compilation and translation of these quotes may be found in Rivera, Tim. References to the fencing treatise of Francisco Román. http://www.spanishsword.org/files/references.roman.pdf (accessed 8/28/2014)
16. Valle, M., Nueva bibliografía. (.411)
17. Valle, M., Nueva bibliografia. p.193
18. Viterbo, S. A esgrima em Portugal. p.44
19. Valle, M. and Curtis, MD., "Un texto de esgrima española del s. XVI". Materiales para la historia del deporte (2009) 7:33-42
20. Pacheco de Narváez, L., Engaño y desengaño. f.49v, f.153v.
21. Vélez de Guevara, L., El diablo cojuelo. f.62r
22. Pacheco de Narváez, L., Nueva Ciencia. p.605
23. Godinho, D.L., Arte de esgrima. f.22r, f.32v, f.46r.
24. Pacheco de Narváez, L., Nueva Ciencia. p.592
25. Pacheco de narváez, L., Grandezas de la espada. f.211
26. Godinho, D.L., Arte de esgrima. f.80r
27. Pacheco de Narváez, L., Nueva Ciencia. p.192, p.670
28. Godinho, D.L. Arte de esgrima. f.103
29. Pacheco de Narváez, L. Engaño y desengaño. f.50v
30. Godinho, D.L. Arte de esgrima. f.83r
31. Pacheco de Narváez, L. Nueva Ciencia. p.499
32. Pacheco de Narváez, L. Nueva Ciencia. p.491
33. Godinho, D.L. Arte de esgrima. f.110r-122r
34. Lhermite, J. Le passetemps de Jehan Lhermite. t.2, p.241
35. Pacheco de Narváez, L. Nueva Ciencia. p.493-494
36. Godinho, D.L Arte de esgrima. f.114v

37. The translation and treatment of the first eleven folios can be found in the Appendix.
38. A transcription and normalization into modern Spanish was published in 2015 by AGEA Editora.
39. It is unknown who Acevedo is.
40. Portuguese. The Lusitanians were an ancient Iberian people of central Portugal, though the name is often used in literary or poetic context to refer to the Portuguese people.
41. Portion illegible
42. Backhand cut.
43. Forehand cut.
44. This is an example of how obtuse many of the marginal notes, some of which are written in a different hand, can be. In this case, the apparent meaning is that, just as a poultice is placed on the wound, the sword should be at the same height as the opponent's attack to counter.
45. Literally "are not as true" (no son tan verdaderos)
46. This refers to the previous chapter; Godinho often uses rule and chapter interchangeably. See regla in the glossary.
47. The word punta is used for both point and thrust, which is the reason for the clarification in the rest of the sentence.
48. romper
49. Romper and rasgar are used interchangeably in the text, and both instances will be translated as ripping.
50. "like how we say zurdo or izquierdo, which are the same thing" (both words refer to the left, or left-handedness)
51. possibly measure or measured
52. palmo – 20 cm or 8 in
53. espada preta
54. That is, to bring an end to the bout, to settle the matter.
55. mesura
56. espada negra
57. librar
58. firmado
59. tentar

60. ganar
61. destreza
62. Tiempos cometidos
63. See glossary.
64. maestros – in other places translated as "master," though more readily understood as "teacher" in these contexts in English.
65. diestros
66. tiempos
67. destreza
68. The montante was often used as a marshal's baton, separating the combatants at the start and end of a bout.
69. Although the phraseology of this paragraph long-sentence is awkward, the meaning is clear: In addition to performing skillfully, the combatants should honor the master's commands, both to begin and to halt, and to quietly endure his criticism, as well as his praise.
70. The abbreviations were found in the original text, but have been replaced in this translation by the words they represent for the ease of the reader. This chapter has been preserved for completeness.
71. tretas
72. tentar
73. palmo – 20 cm or 8 in
74. one who is skilled
75. This chapter number is duplicated in the original.
76. parafusando
77. garatusando
78. "codo, which in Portuguese is called cotovelo" [margin]cotovelo and codo are the same
79. pie de rueda
80. tiempo
81. tiempo
82. codazo
83. tiempos
84. [margin note]"muslo and coxa are the same" (muslo is the Spanish word for thigh,

which is used in the text, while coxa is the Portuguese word)

85. tiempo
86. de arremeso
87. presto – quick, ready
88. diestro
89. tiempo
90. Literally "voided"
91. "canillas, which in another tongue is said canelas"
92. tiempo
93. This chapter number is duplicated in the original.
94. "cogote, which in another tongue is called pescueso"
95. "suelo, which in another tongue is said tierra"
96. arrebatar
97. tiempos
98. f.61 is missing in the numbering
99. "zurdos, which in another tongue are called izquierdos"
100. "muslo, which in another tongue is called coxa"
101. tiempos
102. darle el pecho
103. While "arms" in English generally has the connotation of offensive weaponry, it is used in this text to refer to both offensive and defensive arms.
104. palmo – 20 cm or 8 in
105. "rodilla, which in another tongue they call joelho"
106. reves in the original
107. palmo – 20 cm or 8 in
108. tiempos
109. This chapter and the next are mislabeled in the original – this was marked as "56. Chapter Forty-six," and the next is labeled as "57. Chapter Fifty-seven."
110. maestro mayor
111. como reina – This could mean "as queen" (the shield is queen) or "as it rules."
112. There is no rule six. The manuscript contains the chapter title and nothing below.

113. "izquierdo, which is called zurdo in another tongue"
114. In the original, it says "right foot" instead of "right arm."
115. de puño
116. de aremeso, in chapter 105 of single sword
117. dos palmos – 40 cm or 16 in
118. Literally "in one thought"
119. Literally "in one thought"
120. "lados, which in another tongue is said ilhargas"
121. recoger vel – possibly vela (sail)
122. tiempos
123. possibly a mistake, intending dagger
124. de arremeso
125. de arremeso
126. The meaning here is unclear. Godinho could be saying that there are no feints so you do it this way, or he could be saying that you have to do this in case there are feints.
127. possibly a mistake, intending dagger
128. tiempo
129. encadenado
130. tiempo
131. tiempos
132. Godinho divides the blade into three parts (strong, middle, weak). Here, he is advising that the fingers don't need to go past the guard, out to the first third of the blade.
133. A similar carrying position is illustrated several decades later by the Italian master, Francesco Alfieri in Lo Spadone (1653) Although an Italian, Alfieri teaches the use of the two-handed sword in a series of rules, similar to Godinho and other Iberians.
134. The advice to only use thrusts with the two-handed sword in single combat is also found in the advice of Giacomo di Grassi (1570), who suggests the two-handed sword should only use blows in multiple combat, and thrusts when fighting another of its kind. As Godinho suggests, this advice runs contrary to that of other masters, both Iberian and Italian.
135. This could also mean "in a nails-up position," as Godinho uses the same word for both thrust and point.

136. Godinho uses the same word for both point and thrust, and he his clarifying that he doesn't mean thrust here.

137. Meaning that the cut starts at the opponent on the right side and ends at the opponent on the left side.

138. no es esta la silla adonde se deben asentar – "this is not the chair in which they should sit"

139. Apart from the actual value of the cloak, it also had a symbolic meaning that is evident in several Spanish phrases: "to defend to cloak and sword" (defend tooth and nail, or support at all costs), "to defend your cloak" (look after your home, or rights), "to take someone's cloak" (steal, or take more than what is legal or fair).

140. rastrero – describes something which moves through the air, almost touching the ground

141. Again, Godinho's advice accords with that of other 16th and 17th-century fencing masters, such as Giacomo di Grassi (1570) and Salvator Fabris (1606), that thrusts are not to be used when fighting while surrounded by enemies.

142. You will shout with a loud voice: "Afuera!" – literally "outside!" or "get out!"

143. palmo – 20 cm or 8 in

144. Chapter 124, folio 54

145. In place of the Spanish word for God (dios), this chapter in the original uses a euphemism (vios).

146. onza

147. Carlos I of Spain (1500-1558)

148. François I of France, taken prisoner in the battle of Pavia in 1525.

149. Suleiman I the Magnificent (1494-1566), Ottoman sultan.

150. maestros mayores

151. The Nair or Nayar are a people from the southern Indian state of Kerala. The Portuguese applied the term to all the locals who fought alongside them.

152. tiempo

153. Originally numbered 171, with the last chapter as 172.

154. tiempos

155. These appear at the beginning of the original manuscript, as the folio numbers indicate.

156. tiempo

157. While nearly all of the folios in this list are correct, the chapter numbers correspond

to the numbered paragraphs below, starting on f.7.

158. tiempos
159. tiempos
160. tentar
161. tiempos
162. These appear to be a list of topics that Godinho wished to include, and are crossed off, although not all topics appear in the book.
163. tiempos
164. espada blanca
165. Illegibile, supposed from below and later
166. tiempo
167. tentar
168. See tentar in the glossary; this paragraph discusses other meanings of the word.
169. tiento
170. tentando
171. tentando
172. tiempos
173. Based on the earlier notes corresponding to these paragraphs, what can be surmised to be on the missing page is a discussion of how skill and knowledge are not the same, further discussion of how speed has no place, that withdrawing the foot and stepping back are not the same, that there are true and false blows, and the beginning of how gaining the weak with the strong is false.
174. Possibly the recazo – the unsharpened portion of the blade just beyond the cross.
175. Note that the authors of la verdadera destreza do not use the word treta to mean trick, as Godinho does, but rather to mean a technique which is formed in the mind and executed with an intended outcome; they also refer to their own techniques as tretas.
176. First chapter on two swords, folio 83.
177. Chapter 107 of the sword alone, folio 48.
178. Chapter 154 of the sword alone, folio 54.
179. Chapter 17 of sword and dagger, folio 98.
180. This is shown in Academie de l'Espee, written by Gerard Thibault d'Anvers, published in 1630.

181. Chapter 123, folio 53.

182. Chapter 86 of the sword alone, folio 42.

183. Chapter 41, folio 79.

184. Chapter 128 of the sword alone, folio 55, and chapter 147 of the sword alone, folio 62.

BIBLIOGRAPHY

Leguina y Vidal, Enrique de, *Bibliografía e historia de la esgrima española; apuntes reunidos.* Madrid: [M Beltrán], 1904.

Lhermite, Jehan, *Le Passetemps de Jehan Lhermite.* Atwerpen: J.E. Buschmann, 1896.

Moniz, Jose António, *Inventario secção XIII- Manuscriptos: Collecção Pombalina.* Lisboa : Biblioteca Nacional, 1889.

Pacheco de Narváez, Luis, *Grandezas de la espada.* Madrid: Herederos de Juan Iñiguez de Lequerica, 1600.

_______________, *Engaño y desengaño de los errores que se han querido introducir en la destreza de las armas.* Madrid: Imp. del Reino, 1635.

_______________,*Modo facil y nuevo para examinarse los Maestros en la destreza de las armas y entender sus cien conclusiones*. (Ed. Manuel Valle). Santiago de Compostela: AGEA, 2011.

_______________, *Nueva Ciencia y filosofía de la destreza de las armas*. Madrid: Melchor Sanchez, 1672.

Viterbo, Francisco Marques Sousa, *A esgrima em Portugal. Subsidios para a sua historia.* Lisboa: Manuel Gomes, 1899.

Valle Ortiz, Manuel, *Nueva bibliografía de la antigua esgrima y destreza de las armas.* Santiago de Compostela: AGEA/Edizer, 2012.

Vélez de Guevara, Luis, *El diablo cojuelo*. Madrid: Imp. del Reino, 1641.

Yanguas y Miranda, José, *Diccionario de antigüedades del Reino de Navarra.* Pamplona: Javier Goyeneche, 1840.

9781937439330.